PRAYIN
the JEW,

Recovering the Ancient Roots of New Testament Prayer

Timothy P. Jones, Ed.D.

Lederer Books
a division of
Messianic Jewish Publishers
Clarksville, Maryland

Scripture quotations are taken from the *Complete Jewish Bible*, Copyright © 1998 by David H. Stern, published by Jewish New Testament Publications, Inc. Used by permission.

ISBN-13: 978-1-880226-28-5
ISBN-10: 1-880226-28-6

Library of Congress Control Number: 2005925248
Printed in the United States of America

About the cover—
They entered K'far-Nachum [Capernaum], and on Shabbat [the Sabbath] Yeshua went into the synagogue and began teaching. (Mark 1:21)

The cover photo shows the remains of the ancient synagogue at Capernaum, discovered in the mid-nineteenth century. Capernaum was first established in the second century B.C.E. The ruins pictured were built on the site of an earlier synagogue where Jesus preached. At that time, Capernaum was a large Jewish village and considered to be Yeshua's "own town" (Matt. 9:1), a place where he taught regularly (Luke 4:31).

Lederer Books
a division of
Messianic Jewish Publishers
P.O. Box 615
Clarksville, Maryland 21029

Distributed by
Messianic Jewish Resources International
Order line: (800) 410-7367
E-mail: lederer@messianicjewish.net
Website: www.messianicjewish.net

CONTENTS

For my girl . . .
Hannah Rachel Jones

Hannah, "grace,"
because indeed you are a
gracious gift from God.

Rachel,
because we wept so long for the children
we thought we could not bear,
and God brought you to us
from a distant land.

(Jeremiah 31:15–17)

Lots of silly things have been written about prayer.

Like: "Prayer is a way of lifting ourselves." As if we have the spiritual wherewithal to do that. In fact, the very act of praying is a recognition that we *cannot* lift ourselves.

Or: "Prayer is God's psychotherapy for his children." As if prayer were merely a psychological technique. No, to pray is to enter into a relationship—the most vital relationship that life has to offer.

Or, how about this one: "A prayer in its simplest definition is merely a wish turned Godward." As if prayer were about turning God into a cosmic Santa Claus to fill our wishes. In fact, prayer is most often about learning to *transcend* our self-centered wishes.

And on it goes, a new definition offered with every book on prayer—with a new book and a new definition seeming to come out as often as *Time* magazine. Sadly, many such books, written to tantalize and entertain masses of readers, end up saying things that simply aren't true. And the many that do speak honestly about prayer say little that hasn't been said dozens of times before.

What I like about this book is that it reinforces the great truths of prayer while providing a fresh look at the topic. And the fresh take is not just Timothy Jones' idiosyncratic, very personal way of looking at prayer. Instead, it is grounded in a substantive examination of the life of Jesus.

Over the last few decades, New Testament scholars have made many remarkable discoveries about daily Jewish life in first-century Israel. We now know a great deal about how a person like Jesus, raised in the devout home of a skilled laborer, would have been taught to pray. We have a pretty good idea about the very prayers he would have used in synagogue services, at home, while traveling, or when visiting the Temple in Jerusalem. Jones has done us a service by helping us to see, through historically grounded vignettes and careful explanations, what Jesus' prayer life would have been like.

Many today wear bracelets, T-shirts, and a thousand other trinkets that have emblazoned on them the phrase: "What would Jesus do?" The idea is to let that question guide all our actions. So why not apply it to prayer? "How would Jesus pray?" Jones not only replies to that question, but also answers the logical follow-up questions: So what? In light of Jesus' prayers, how should we, his followers, adapt his prayer life to ours—or, more precisely, how should we adapt *our* prayer life to his?

For Jesus' followers, prayer is like breathing. This is a book designed to help readers "breathe deeply" as they enter into prayer. To be sure, this is not the last word on prayer. Nor are readers obligated to sign off on everything any author says about a topic that is ultimately a mystery. Yet, if Jones, as a result of alerting us to Jesus' prayer life, does nothing more than to give us a broader, deeper, and richer context to our prayers, we'll all "breathe" a little bit easier.

—Mark Galli
Managing Editor, *Christianity Today*

> During Yeshua's life on earth, he offered up prayers and
> petitions, crying aloud and shedding tears, to the One
> who had the power to deliver him from death; and he
> was heard because of his godliness. . . . Consequently, he
> is totally able to deliver those who approach God
> through him; since he is alive forever and thus forever
> able to intercede on their behalf. (Hebrews 5:7; 7:25)

During his time on the earth, Yeshua (Jesus) prayed persistently
(Luke 5:16). He prayed desperately (Heb. 5:7). Two thousand
years later, he hasn't stopped praying. In fact, according to the
author of Hebrews, he *lives to* pray, and he expects us to follow his
example. No other religion in history includes a Supreme Being
that prays—let alone a God who "is alive forever . . . to intercede"
for his people (see Heb. 7:25).

What I find even more amazing is that Yeshua *learned* to pray.
He didn't emerge from his mother's womb with a prayer journal
in one fist and a fountain pen in the other. Yeshua was equally
divine and human. That means he learned to pray in the same way
that your children learn to pray—by imitating the prayers that he
heard. For Yeshua, these were primarily the prayers of the
synagogue, the Temple, and centuries of Jewish tradition.

Unfortunately, many have never even heard the prayers that
Yeshua learned and loved. In some sense, that limits our
understanding of the Father who listened so intently to the
prayers of his Son. This book has been written in order to
introduce you to the prayers that Yeshua prayed. Some of these
prayers of Yeshua are recorded in the Hebrew Scriptures. Others
are drawn from Jewish tradition. A few appear only in the *B'rit
Hadashah* (New Testament). Yet, each of them was shaped by the
prayers that Yeshua learned and prayed at home, in the
synagogue, and in the Temple.

Each chapter begins with an imaginative retelling of an event
from the life of Yeshua. These fictional narratives weave the
original context and culture of the prayers into the biblical stories
in order to help you not only study the prayers, but also

experience them. You will begin your journey in the Temple, overhearing a prayer that echoed within its walls when the infant Yeshua arrived there in his mother's arms. Later, you will become a guest at a wedding in Cana, a learner wandering the hills of Galilee, a mourner at a funeral in Bethany, then a nameless bystander on the Hill of the Skull.

Where will your journey end? I don't know. That's up to you. My hope is that *Praying Like the Jew, Jesus* will enrich your prayer life—and even more, that it will renew your understanding of the Father to whom Yeshua prayed.

FUNCTION OR LIFESTYLE?

Before beginning this journey, let's look at one more question: What separates the prayers that Yeshua heard and learned from the prayers that we typically pray? For many, prayer tends to be a *function*—an instrument to receive something from God. In the life of Yeshua, prayer was not merely a *function*; it was a *lifestyle*. Prayer punctuated every chore, every ritual, every daily task. Whenever first-century Jewish people rolled out of bed in the morning, whenever they washed their hands, whenever they lit a candle, whenever they drank, whenever they ate, whenever they glimpsed a rainbow, they whispered a prayer. Many of the prayers were single sentences. Most were recited in specific ways.

These prayers were not spoken merely because someone had needs that God could fulfill; these prayers were prayed because the Jewish people lived every part of their lives as people who were united with God through an unbreakable covenant. Prayer was not merely a means to receive something from God; it was a persistent expression of their life *in* God. The Hebrew term *tefillah* (prayer) has nothing to do with receiving anything from God. The central implication of *tefillah* is "to discern what is in oneself."

That's why, as you reflect on these prayers, it isn't only your understanding of prayer that will increase. Your discernment of God and his relationship with you will grow too. You will begin to see your heavenly Father and his plan not through the lenses of tradition and theology, but through the eyes of his Son. You will experience . . .

. . . a God who delights in doing the unexpected.
. . . a God who goes beyond our expectations.
. . . a God whose deepest desire is to create a community that reflects his glory.
. . . a God who longs to create a new future for this community.

A WORD ABOUT FORMAT, SOURCES, AND TERMINOLOGY

Reconstructing the Jewish worship practices of the first century is extremely difficult. None of the written records of these prayers is from that time. Many references are from the Middle Ages—hundreds of years after Yeshua's earthly ministry. Some phrases in the available records reflect reactions to the emergence of Messianic faith and to the destruction of the Jewish Temple in 70 C.E.

As such, reconstructing the first-century form of these prayers entails equal amounts of in-depth research and educated guesswork. The liturgies I have reconstructed may not be identical to the words with which Yeshua was familiar. Nevertheless, I have carefully researched every rendering, and I am confident that these reconstructions are reasonably similar to the prayers Yeshua knew.

In their prayers and public reading of Scripture, ancient Hebrews substituted *ADONAI* ('Supreme Lord") or *HaShem* ("the Name") for YHVII, the unspeakable name of God, which is related to the Hebrew phrase *Ehyeh*, or "I AM". Although the holy name is rendered "LORD" in most English Bibles, in my reconstructions of the ancient liturgies I have used "*ADONAI*." The purpose is to remind the reader that, although the word spoken in these prayers meant "Lord," the implication of the word was the ineffable, holy name of God.

In keeping with the book's focus on the Jewish context of the first century, many Hebrew and Aramaic terms appear in the text. So, for example, "Yeshua" is used instead of the Anglicized Latin name "Jesus," "Miryam" appears instead of "Mary," and so on. I have provided a glossary of many Hebrew and Aramaic terms in the back of the book.

PART I

Knowing the God Who
Delights in the Unexpected

The Redemption of Israel arrives in swaddling bands.
The Creator blesses his creation from an execution stake.
The Suffering Servant begins his ministry at a wedding
   feast.

Unexpected   incarnation!
Unexpected   humiliation!
Unexpected   jubilation!

Could anyone but God ever have concocted such scheme?
Could anyone but God ever have made it work?
Could anyone but God ever have delighted in making
   it work?

Chapter One

Unexpected Answers—
Embracing the God Who Surprises

PRAYERS OF EXPECTATION

Speedily cause the offspring of your servant David to flourish, and let him be exalted by your saving power, for we wait all day long for your salvation. Blessed are you, *Adonai*, who causes salvation to flourish.

> *Malkhut beyt David* (Kingship of the House of David)
> Fifteenth *B'rakhah* (blessing) of the *Amidah*

There was in Yerushalayim [Jerusalem] a man named Shim'on [Simeon]. This man was a *tzaddik* [righteous person], he was devout, he waited eagerly for God to comfort Isra'el, and the *Ruach HaKodesh* [the Holy Spirit] was upon him. It had been revealed to him by the *Ruach HaKodesh* that he would not die before he had seen the Messiah of ADONAI. Prompted by the Spirit, he went into the Temple courts; and when the parents brought in the child Yeshua to do for him what the *Torah* required, Shim'on took him in his arms, made a *b'rakhah* to God, and said, "Now, ADONAI, according to your word, your servant is at peace as you let him go; for I have seen with my own eyes your *yeshu'ah* [salvation], which you prepared in the presence of all peoples—a light that will bring revelation to the *Goyim* [nations] and glory to your people Isra'el."

Yeshua's father and mother were marvelling at the things Shim'on was saying about him. Shim'on blessed them and said to the child's mother, Miryam [Mary], "This child will cause many in Isra'el to fall and to rise, he will become a sign whom people will speak against; moreover, a sword will pierce your own heart too. All this will happen in order to reveal many people's inmost thoughts."

There was also a prophet named Hannah Bat-P'nu'el [Anna, daughter of Phanuel], of the tribe of Asher. She was a very old woman—she had lived with her husband seven years after her marriage and had remained a widow ever since; now she was eighty-four. She never left the Temple grounds but worshipped there night and day, fasting and praying. She came by at that moment and began thanking God and speaking about the child to everyone who was waiting for Yerushalayim to be liberated. When Yosef [Joseph] and Miryam had finished doing everything required by the *Torah* of ADONAI, they returned to Galilee, to their town Natzeret [Nazareth]. The child grew and became strong and filled with wisdom—God's favor was upon him. (Luke 2:25–40)

The rising sun threw a ruddy glow across the eastern walls of the Holy City. The ancient ramparts overshadowed two pilgrims, a man and a teenage girl, as they trudged up the western slope of the Kidron Valley. They ducked through the Ashpot Gate, at the southeast corner of the city. Already, merchants had clustered along the dusty streets to hawk dried figs and salted fish, fresh olives and fist-sized lumps of bread.

When they reached the Temple courts, Miryam handed a swaddled bundle of life to her husband. She slipped through a gate into the Court of Women. Thirteen bronze chests lined the court. The girl's meager handful of coins—the price of two turtle-doves—clattered pitifully in the trumpet-shaped opening in the third chest.

From the chests, Miryam made her way up the stairs toward the Court of Israel. She peered through the Beautiful Gate into the Temple and drank in the beauty of the massive doors, the marble pillars, the great stone altar. Her eyes traced the snowy pillars and the billows of smoke upward until they seemed to merge with the highest heaven. As Miryam remembered the words of the white-robed messenger—"he will be great, he will be called Son of the High God"—she repeated the familiar line from the *Amidah*: "Speedily cause the offspring of your servant David to flourish, and let him be exalted by your saving power, for we wait all day long for your salvation." As soon as her child learned to speak, he too would learn to pray for the salvation of Israel. And, perhaps—if she had correctly understood God's messenger—he would *become* the salvation of Israel.

One of the priests reached into a wooden cage and grasped a dove by its neck. The bird's wings thrashed wildly and its delicate coo escalated into a frantic warble. Suddenly the priest's hands jerked. The bird's neck cracked, and the sound echoed throughout the Court of the Priests. Miryam winced as warm blood spattered the corner of the altar and ran along its base. The dove was her sin offering—the offering for her unholiness, for her failures, for her sins.

Another priest severed the second dove's head and pitched it into a smoldering mass of wood atop the altar. Blood trickled unevenly down the side of the altar as the priest tore out the bird's entrails and tossed them into the ash heap. He threw what was left of the dove into the fire on the altar.[1] The sacrifice for Miryam's purification was over. Now, it was time for the *pidyon ha'ben*, the redemption of the firstborn.[2]

When Miryam turned around, Yosef was already beside her. The priest who stood with him was ancient, with a snowy beard and eyes that seemed to stare beyond the Temple courts. He smiled at Miryam and Yosef and said simply, "I am Simeon."

Yosef lifted the child and spoke: "This is my firstborn son, the firstborn of his mother, and the Holy One has commended us to redeem him. As it is written, 'Set aside for me all the firstborn. Whatever is first from the womb among the people of Isra'el, both of humans and of animals, belongs to me,' and, 'Everything that comes first out of the womb, of all living things which they offer to Adonai, whether human or animal, will be yours. However, the firstborn of a human being you must redeem.'"[3]

Simeon clasped the child in his trembling arms and asked, "Would you rather give me your firstborn son, the firstborn of his mother, or redeem him for five shekels of silver?" "I want to redeem my son," answered Yosef, as he withdrew a leather pouch from his belt. "Here are the shekels for his redemption." Simeon held the pouch above the child's head and looked upward. "This instead of that," he intoned. "The shekels instead of the child. This in exchange for that. This in remission of that. May this child enter into life, into the *Torah*, and into the fear of heaven." At this point, the liturgy ended.[4] Yet, Simeon continued in a voice that burned with undiluted joy: "Blessed be Adonai our God, king of the universe! Now, Adonai, according to your word, your servant is at peace as you let him go; for I have seen with my own eyes your salvation, which you prepared in the presence of all peoples—a light that will bring revelation to the nations and glory to your people Isra'el!"

Miryam and Yosef stood silent. They could not escape the intent of Simeon's words: This baby . . . the Messiah? The revelation of the living God? Before the dumbfounded couple could respond, Simeon placed a grizzled hand on the infant's forehead and conferred the ancient blessing on them: "May Adonai bless you and keep you. May Adonai make his face shine on you and show you his favor. May Adonai lift his face toward you and give you peace."[5]

Suddenly, a shadow passed across Simeon's face. His eyes clouded as he looked into the wide eyes of the girl who had borne this baby. "This child," he said, "will cause many in Isra'el to fall and to rise, he will become a sign whom people will speak against; moreover"—the priest's lips trembled—"a sword will pierce your own heart too."

Simeon gazed one last time into the infant's watery, wondering eyes before handing the child to Yosef. Miryam and Yosef walked silently down the steps that led from the Temple's Beautiful Gate into the Court of Women. Despite the crowds around them, they felt cold, alone.

An unexpected shout wrenched the couple from their bewildered trance: "All who eagerly await the redemption of Jerusalem, hear me! Blessed be ADONAI, for you have made your face shine upon your people and redeemed them!" It was a gnarled old woman, howling in sheer ecstasy, whirling like a teenaged bride with a walking stick. She repeated her refrain again, "All who eagerly await the redemption of Jerusalem, hear me! Blessed be ADONAI, for you have made your face shine upon your people and redeemed them!"

The crowds around the old woman parted like the Red Sea. She was heading directly toward Miryam and Yosef. She waved a bony finger at the bundle that Yosef clutched against his chest. "All who eagerly await the redemption of Jerusalem, hear me," she declared in quavering voice. "This child, this child, is the redemption of Jerusalem!"

Surely, the old woman's words seemed like insanity—the redemption of Jerusalem, wrapped in swaddling bands? Miryam did not know whether to laugh at the absurdity of a redeemer who couldn't control his own bowels or to cry at the sword that would pierce her own heart. In the end, she did both.

UNIMAGINABLE GLORY, IMPLAUSIBLE PACKAGE

Who would have believed that a girl with one foot still in puberty would soon have her other foot in motherhood—without placing either foot in a man's bed? Who would have guessed? It's the recognition that "God's 'nonsense' is wiser than humanity's 'wisdom.' And God's 'weakness' is stronger than humanity's 'strength'" (1 Cor. 1:25). That's precisely what Simeon and Hannah experienced when Miryam arrived in the Temple to offer the sacrifice for her purification.

For decades, Simeon and Hannah had waited expectantly for the crown prince of Israel to ride into the Temple courts. Every *Shabbat* (Sabbath), they turned their faces toward the heavens and recited a familiar prayer.[6] Because they stood when they prayed this prayer, it became known as the *Amidah* (literally, "Standing"). The closing lines of the *Amidah* included a prayer of expectation—a prayer asking God to establish his Messianic Kingdom: "Speedily cause the offspring of your servant David to flourish, and let him be exalted by your saving power, for we wait all day long for your salvation. Blessed are you, *Adonai*, who causes salvation to flourish."[7]

A later rabbi expanded on this expectation of the Messiah:

> If a king will arise from David's house who is learned in *Torah* and observant of the commands of the *Torah*, as prescribed by the written law and the oral law, as David his ancestor was, and will compel all of *Israel* to walk in the way of the *Torah* and repair the breaches in their observance of the *Torah*; and fight the wars of God, we may, with assurance, consider him the Messiah.[8]

An obscure prayer from the Dead Sea Scrolls describes the expectations for the Messianic age even more clearly: "Blessed be *Adonai*. . . . You will cause the wicked to be our ransom and the faithless to be our redemption. You will wipe out all our oppressors, and we will praise your name forever."[9]

The people's expectations for the Messiah were clear: He would be a descendant of King David, and he would establish his Kingdom through political power and military might. As far as we know, that's the kind of Messiah that Simeon and Hannah expected too. Instead, they got a swaddled tot who looked like every other infant they had ever seen.

This infant may have been from the house of David, but he didn't enjoy royal wealth; his mother offered a bargain-basement bird as her sacrifice instead of a lamb. When it came to wiping out the oppressors of Israel, the baby wasn't very well equipped, either. He didn't have a gallant stallion, he was too small to wear armor, and the only sword in his grasp was the one that would pierce his mother's heart.

Yet somehow, Simeon and Hannah recognized this infant as the Messiah. Hannah declared that he was "the redemption of Jerusalem"—the one who would end the bondage of Israel.[10] For centuries, prayers for the Messiah had revolved around royal rulers and revolutions. In the midst of these misapprehensions, Simeon spoke another prayer of expectation—a prayer that revolved around the revelation of God in the least likely place, in the tender flesh of a peasant's baby: "I have seen with my own eyes your *yeshu'ah*, which you prepared in the presence of all peoples— a light that will bring revelation to the *Goyim* and glory to your people Isra'el."

"Light" and "salvation," he called this infant. These words marked this baby as the Messiah (see Isa. 52:10–13; 62:11), but they also marked him as something greater. Centuries earlier the psalmist had written, "ADONAI is my light and salvation." The prophets echoed, "God is my salvation" and "though I live in the dark, ADONAI is my light" (Ps. 27:1; Isa. 12:2; Mic. 7:8). Simeon saw no flash of glory, and he heard no heavenly voices. Yet he searched the face of this wriggling infant and somehow knew that his hands were cradling the Redeemer of Israel. He was so certain of this infant's identity that he could whisper to God, "Your servant is at peace."

Somehow, not even the utterly implausible package of an infant's flesh could conceal the unimaginable glory that Simeon glimpsed in this baby. He recognized that the child was the answer to his prayer of expectation: "Speedily cause the offspring of your servant David to flourish, and let him be exalted by your saving power."

SEEING GOD'S SALVATION

If I had been standing in Simeon's sandals, I suspect that I would have given up on the arrival of God's Messiah long before Yeshua showed up in the Court of Women. When Miryam and Yosef made their way to Jerusalem, hypocrisy and corruption reigned in the Temple courts. King Herod frequently appointed high priests according to his personal whims. The Essenes became so frustrated with the corruption that they withdrew to a desert compound near the Dead Sea. The Zealots formed a political coalition and tried to force the coming of God's Kingdom through violence.

Still, Simeon and Hannah never gave up on the promise of God's presence among his people. According to Luke, Simeon did not go to the gathering-place of God's people only because it was his job. He went because he was "prompted by the Spirit." Hannah the prophetess "never left the Temple grounds but worshipped there night and day, fasting and praying" (Luke 2:27–38). Why? The worn-out priest and the half-crazy prophetess had embraced the notion that God was still working—even in the midst of the corruption that surrounded them. So, they were able to look past the implausible packaging and recognize the divine Messiah. Simeon and Hannah hadn't merely prayed for God's Messiah. They fully expected that God would answer their prayers, and they were willing to embrace an answer that didn't quite fit what they had so long expected—a little boy whose mother would teach him to pray the *Amidah* long before either the boy or his mother fully realized how he would answer his people's pleas.

LIVING THE PRAYERS

If prayers of expectation truly became something that we chose to live by, instead of past relics that we repeat from time to time, the world's definition of "power" wouldn't survive very long. Faithful followers of God had long prayed, "Cause the offspring of your servant David to flourish, and let him be exalted by your saving power." And God did. But God's definition of "saving power" didn't require political posturing or military might. God's definition of power entailed meekness, humility, and humiliation—the meekness of an infant, the humility of a carpenter, and the humiliation of a stake of execution. In *The Hungering Dark*, novelist Frederick Buechner reminds us how God came to earth:

> He came in such a way that we can always turn him down, as we could crack the baby's skull like an eggshell or nail him up when he gets too big for that. God comes to us in the hungry man that we do not have to feed, comes to us in the lonely man we do not have to comfort, comes to us in all the desperate human need of people everywhere that we are always free to turn our backs upon.[11]

Still, God's people persist in defining God's presence in terms of human power. Suppose one of your friends said, "See that person? The power of God is really with her!" What would you expect to see? A frightened teenager with a hungry baby at her breast and a worried husband at her side? Probably not. Yet, this was precisely the sort of person who carried the answer to the prayers of expectation into the courtyard of the Temple. In the words of Miryam, "[He] has taken notice of his servant-girl in her humble position! ... [He] brought down rulers from their thrones, raised up the humble" (Luke 1:48, 52). It didn't make sense, but it's the truth.

THE PROMISE OF THE GOD WHO SURPRISES

God loves to reveal his presence among his people. But he has a penchant for revealing his power through the least likely pathways—through humility and simplicity, powerlessness and humiliation. And yet, when we are willing to wait and to watch for God's glory amid the powerlessness of his people, we eventually find ourselves praying with Simeon, "I have seen with my own eyes your *yeshu'ah*" in the very places where the world sees only weakness.

Who knows? The reeking alcoholic who barely made it into the building could end up leading your congregation's recovery program. That new member who cackles constantly? She may be the greatest prayer warrior in your entire congregation. The junior-high kid who's struggling with the notion of deodorant? Could be he'll be working with the youth in a few years. And you? If God can come to earth as a little screecher in the nursery at Bethlehem, I'm sure he can do something with you, too.

That's the promise of the God who surprises us.

A MEDITATION

Master,
my eyes have seen your salvation.
It doesn't make sense, but it works.
Yet sometimes I still catch myself
expecting you to reveal yourself
in ways that make sense to me . . .
expecting you to redeem the people that *I* would redeem . . .
expecting salvation to occur on my terms.
I forget that it's *"your* salvation"—not mine.
I have a hard time
waiting for
watching for
longing for
your salvation . . .
your revelation . . .
your way of doing things.
My plans make so much more sense,
but they fall apart so quickly.
Your plans take so long
and seem so strange and so weak,
but they last forever.
Help me to watch and to wait for you.

Chapter Two

Unexpected Vulnerability—
Embracing the God Who Risks

PRAYERS OF BLESSING

Blessed be *Adonai* our God, king of the universe, he who has sanctified us according to his commandments and commanded us concerning the washing of hands.

Traditional Jewish Blessing

Blessed be *Adonai* our God, king of the universe who brings forth bread from the earth.

Traditional Jewish Blessing

Yochanan Bar-Z'kharyah [John, son of Zechariah] rubbed his eyes and peered over Yosef's sleeping form. His cousin's space on the floor was already vacant, his bedding piled against the wall. Yochanan quickly rolled his mat and tiptoed out of the guestroom. As he slipped outside, three blasts from a ram's horn pierced the spring air. The daily lots had been cast in the Temple. The priests were preparing to offer the morning sacrifices and burn the incense. Within minutes, the scents of seared flesh and incense would saturate the eastern half of the Holy City.

Yochanan searched the walled courtyard behind the house before glancing toward the roof. There, he saw his cousin Yeshua sitting on the edge of the house, watching the sun peek over the Mount of Olives. Yochanan scrambled up the steps and flopped down, beside Yeshua.

"What are—?" Yochanan began.

"Sssshhh! Listen . . ."

Jangling timbrels and chanting voices resonated from the Temple courts. The Levites were singing the *hallel* psalms[1]—the songs of praise—just as they did every morning. Yochanan was still trying to decipher which portion they were chanting when Yeshua began to recite the words with them:

> The very rock that the builders rejected
> has become the cornerstone!
> This has come from ADONAI,
> and in our eyes it is amazing.
> This is the day . . .

"Yochanan! Yeshua!"

Yosef's voice interrupted the recitation. The cousins clambered down the stairs and into the guestroom. Elisheva [Elizabeth], Miryam, and the younger children were already gone. Yochanan's father Z'kharyah still lay in the corner of the guestroom, snoring loudly. Last night he had told them the story about the messenger who had appeared in the Temple to announce Yochanan's birth. He told the same story every year when the family gathered here, in the ancestral home of Z'kharyah's family, for the *Pesach* (Passover) celebration. After hearing it for twelve years, Yeshua was quite certain that he could remember the story without Z'kharyah's help, but he had listened to the old priest anyway. This afternoon every priest, even aged Z'kharyah, would gather at the Temple to offer nearly 600,000 lambs—one for each family that made the pilgrimage to Jerusalem.

When Ya'akov [James], Shim'on [Simon], and little Yosef[2] returned with Elisheva and Miryam, Yeshua and Yochanan followed Yosef behind the house. As they clustered around the dung pit, Yosef told Yeshua, "My son, now you are old enough to take the responsibility for keeping the covenant and the commandments. Today, you will speak the blessings and recite the *Sh'ma* [the central confession of Jewish faith]. Today, you will wear *tzitziyot* [fringes] and *t'fillin* [phylacteries].[3] Today you will enter the Court of Israel together to offer the sacrifices. For today, you begin to take the yoke of the *Torah* upon yourself."[4]

Z'kharyah hobbled around a bush to join Yosef, Yeshua, and Yochanan, and intoned in a gravelly voice, "Embrace the *Torah* with joy, Yeshua. It is your life. Its commandments are not too hard or too far away. No, the word is in your mouth and in your heart for you to obey. The *Torah* is as a well-made yoke upon the ox's shoulders—it brings pain only when the ox struggles against it. If you obey its precepts, the yoke of *Torah* will be easy, my son, and its burden will be light."[5]

The twelve-year-old Yeshua and his cousin scraped some dirt into the dung pit before turning toward the massive jars that stood beside the house. Yeshua gasped as he plunged his hands into one of the jars. The waters of purification always seemed as frigid as the snow on Mount Hermon. He scrubbed each of his palms with the opposite fist until Yosef nodded to him. Yeshua nodded silently, pondering his great-uncle's words. He drew a deep breath and spoke the blessing: "Blessed be *Adonai* our God, king of the universe, he who has sanctified us according to his commandments and commanded us concerning the washing of hands."

Yosef, Yeshua, Z'kharyah, and Yochanan went back in the house and joined the women and children on a woven mat on the floor. Miryam had filled two bowls with dried figs and clumps of curds. Conversation and laughter, stimulated by memories of Passovers past, flowed freely within the little circle—until Z'kharyah raised his quavering hands.

Even Ya'akov and little Yosef hushed as the elder spoke: "Last *Pesach*, my son, Yochanan, the child of my old age, took upon himself the responsibility to keep the covenant. This *Pesach*, Yeshua begins to prepare himself to become a son of the commandments. Today, he will speak the blessings and the *Sh'ma*."

Yeshua looked downward and recited the blessing for the food, "Blessed be *Adonai* our God, king of the universe, who brings forth bread from the earth." Everyone in the room—except baby Shim'on, who lay in his mother's arms nursing noisily—murmured in unison, "Amen."

As he spoke, Miryam gazed into her ~~oldest~~ son's dark, brooding eyes. He looked so normal, so . . . ordinary. Yet she, more than anyone else, knew that Yeshua had never been ordinary. His penetrating questions still unnerved her. The uncertainty of his future terrified her. "A sword will pierce your own heart," the priest Simeon had murmured to her years earlier, and she sensed the twist of the sword again as she searched her boy's eyes and wondered who this child would become.

Yeshua's voice disrupted her thoughts. When Yeshua began to recite the *Sh'ma*, Miryam softly murmured the words in unison with him:

> *Sh'ma, Yisra'el! Adonai Eloheinu, Adonai echad*
> [Hear, Isra'el! *Adonai* our God, *Adonai* is one] . . .

Before Yeshua continued, the family whispered together, "Blessed be the Name of his glorious Kingdom for ever and ever."

> . . . and you are to love *Adonai* your God with all your heart, all your being, and all your resources. These words, which I am ordering you today, are to be on your heart; and you are to teach them carefully to your children. You are to talk about them when you sit at home, when you are traveling on the road, when you lie down and when you get up. Tie them on your hand as a sign, put them at the front of a headband around your forehead, and write them on the door-frames of your house and on your gates. (Deut. 6:4–9)

Yeshua paused before speaking the blessing that marked the end of the *Sh'ma*: "Blessed be *Adonai* our God. His word to us is true and firm, forever and ever, unto all generations. Blessed be *Adonai*—he who has redeemed Israel. Amen"[6]

Utter silence had flooded the guestroom. Yeshua had not recited the words of the *Sh'ma* as if he believed them to be true. He had spoken them as if he *knew* they were true, as if the words did not flow from an ancient scroll, but from his own heart. And the sword wrenched within Miryam again as she ached to understand this child whom she loved so desperately but who never truly seemed to belong to her.

Finally, the voice of Z'kharyah splintered the silence. "Son of Miryam." He placed his hand on Yeshua's shoulder and gently blessed him, "May A DONAI bless you and keep you. May A DONAI make his face shine on you and show you his favor. May A DONAI lift up his face toward you and give you peace."

WHY BLESSED?

As a faithful first-century Jew, the words "Blessed[7] be *Adonai*" would have punctuated every aspect of Yeshua's life. Before he ate, after he ate, when he plunged his hands into the waters of purification, when he saw a rainbow, when he put on *t'fillin*, each week when the celebration of the *Shabbat* ended, before and after he recited the *Sh'ma*,[8] Yeshua spoke the words, "Blessed be *Adonai*." And it wasn't only when Yeshua recited the prayers of his ancestors that the word "blessed" touched his life. When his mother showed up on Elisheva's front porch, Elisheva cried, "How blessed are you among women! And how blessed is the child in your womb!" When one of Yeshua's followers stumbled into a recognition of his rabbi's identity, Yeshua declared, "Shim'on Bar-Yochanan, . . . how blessed you are!" When clusters of squirming children clamored to be cuddled by the miracle-worker from Nazareth, Yeshua gathered them into his arms and "made a *b'rakhah* [blessing] over them." On the night of his betrayal, Yeshua "took the *matzah* [unleavened bread], made the *b'rakhah*, broke it, and handed it to them." His final earthly act was to bless the women and men who stuck around long enough to see him return to his Father. It was while he was blessing them that his Father welcomed him home (see Matt. 14:19; 16:17; Mark 10:16; Luke 1:42–45; 24:30, 51).

What, though, does it mean to speak a blessing, to make a *b'rakhah*? The verbal root of *barukh*—the Hebrew word usually translated "bless"—means literally "to bow." The noun form means "knee," as in "bow the knee." So, if I truly bless someone, I do not merely wish him well; I bow to him. I submit to him. I give myself to him. In short, I become vulnerable.

When we sing, "Bless the Lord, oh my soul" or "Blessed be *Adonai*," we are admitting that we are bound not only to offer *our praises* to God but also to offer *ourselves*.[9] When we ask God to bless us, we acknowledge something even greater—we recognize God's desire to give his own self to us. Through those words, we confess that our God is willing to become vulnerable for the sake of his people.

THE VULNERABILITY OF BLESSEDNESS

God's longing to give himself to humanity is as ancient as the Garden of Eden. In the garden, he refused to keep the joy of creating new life to himself—on Adam and Eve's wedding night, "God blessed them: God said to them, 'Be fruitful and multiply, fill the earth'" (Gen. 1:28). In the Exodus, he refused to retain the satisfaction of ownership for himself—he blessed a band of former pyramid-builders with a land that flowed with milk and honey (see Deut. 26:6–9; 28:3–6). In the incarnation, he even refused to keep heaven to himself—he came down to earth and risked our rejection to populate his presence with the likes of you and me.

And, oh how he "came down!" He encased his deity in a microscopic embryo that grew for nine months beneath the heart of a peasant girl. "His last true comfort was that final moment before slipping from his mother's womb. Then, a borrowed feeding trough met him, and the story of his pain began."[10] He had emerged in an insignificant corner of the Roman Empire as a baby who couldn't speak or eat solid food or control his bladder.[11] He endured puberty! His hometown was in the province of Galilee. "As Cajun Country is to New Orleans and Kerry is to Dublin, the Galilean hills were the ultimate Boonies, the archetypical setting for all of arch Jerusalem's hayseed jokes."[12]

Through his incarnation in Yeshua the Messiah, God embraced the deepest degree of vulnerability. God blessed his creation in the most indisputable way. And at the intersection of two blood soaked beams of wood, the full meaning of blessedness became painfully clear. For on that Roman stake of execution, the omnipotent Creator submitted to the pain of a shattered world and demonstrated once and for all, what it means to be a blessing.

BLESSINGS AND FAVORS

Still, God's people consistently forget the meaning of blessedness, confusing *blessings* with *favors*. Pay close attention to the difference: A favor is a cheap, short-lived present, usually given out of duty (think of a "party favor"). A blessing, on the other hand, is a conscious choice to open oneself to the possibility of pain and rejection. I can do a favor for someone and risk nothing. Not so when I bless someone. By commanding the Israelites to repeat the words, "May ADONAI bless you," God was not merely demonstrating his good favor toward them. He was also declaring that he had chosen to become vulnerable for their sakes. He was expressing his willingness to risk rejection at the hands of his own people.

On the surface, we believe that God wants to bless us—at least that's what we claim. Yet, beneath our comfortable cloaks of creeds and curricula and confessions of faith, I suspect that most of us still believe that God operates according to the same rules as our world—a system in which we give favors to earn favors. Like a spoiled brat in a toy store, we assume that if we have done our chores ("I read through the Scriptures again this year!") and if we ask politely ("I pray this in your name"), our Father will give us the favors that we want. In the process, we miss completely what it means to bless and to be blessed.

When we believe that God interacts with humanity according to a system of favors, one of two things happens: Some people come to believe that they can do enough favors to earn God's favor. They are fooling themselves. Others recognize that they can never do enough favors to earn God's favor, but they still run themselves ragged trying. These folks attend every committee meeting, teach every class, and fix every leaky faucet in their congregation's building. They are the women and men who do so many favors for God's people that they never learn to receive and rejoice in God's blessings. They work to earn a love they already possess and are terrified of forfeiting a love they can never lose.

There is, however, another group of people, those that Yeshua called the "poor in spirit" (Matt. 5:3). These folks recognize that they have nothing to offer God. More importantly, they realize that what God craves from us is not a statistical increase in our number of good deeds. What he wants is *us*, prepared to be transformed and stripped of our pitiful attempts to impress him.

Even greater, what God wants to give to us is not a string of cosmic party favors—a bit more prestige in one part of our lives, fewer problems in another. God commanded his people to speak the words, "May ADONAI bless you," because he longed to give his children the gift of himself. Blessedness is not about receiving things; it is about receiving God. To receive the blessing of God's presence is to rejoice in God not because he does favors *for us*, but because he has shared his own sacred identity *with us*.

BECOMING THE BLESSING

There's a catch when it comes to receiving God's blessing, though: "I will bless you, and I will make your name great," God informed Abram, "and you are to be a blessing" (Gen. 12:2). If I have truly received God's blessing, I must become the blessing of God to the people around me—and becoming a blessing isn't easy. Simon Peter described the blessed life in this way: The blessed life means "not repaying evil with evil or insult with insult, but, on the contrary, with blessing. For it is to this that you have been called, so that you might receive a blessing" (1 Pet. 3:9). When I become the blessing of God, I respond to every event in my life according to a set of values that differs radically from the world around me.

I refuse to allow the opinions of others to erode my joy, because my Father has given himself to me and he is the Source of Delight.

I refuse to seek revenge, because my Father has given himself to me and he is the judge of the universe.

I refuse to keep track of others' faults, because my Father has refused to keep track of mine.

If I become this sort of person, the bad news is that I can end up hurt. The good news is that I no longer care where I end up, because I have found my joy and value not in myself or in my circumstances but in my God.

It isn't easy to live a life of blessedness. Frankly, becoming the blessing of God can cause pain . . . deep pain. For, when I become God's blessing, I am forced to recognize the full breath of my own selfishness. How often have I refused to say to a someone who has wronged me, "If I have offended you, please forgive me?" How often have I longed to weep while praying with a friend who was hurting—but fought the tears until my temples throbbed rather than risk the appearance of being weak? How often have I sat piously in my seat during a time of worship while my mind flitted from one self-centered fantasy to another?

To refuse to hold a grudge against the other person was a favor; to ask for forgiveness would have been a blessing.

To pray with my friend was a favor; to weep with him or her would have been a blessing.

To gather with God's people was a favor; to submit my entire being to God would have been a blessing.

Becoming a blessing means self-sacrifice; Yeshua is our example.

NECESSARY, BUT NOT EASY

Let's not deceive ourselves: The life of blessing is embarrassing, offensive, and risky. If we call ourselves followers of the Messiah, it is also absolutely necessary. Brennan Manning puts it this way:

> The love of our God isn't dignified at all, and apparently that's the way He expects our love to be. Not only does He require that we accept His inexplicable, embarrassing kind of love, but once we've accepted it, He expects us to behave the same way with others. I suppose I could live, if I had to, with a God whose love for us is embarrassing, but the thought that I've got to act that way with other people—that's a bit too much to swallow.[13]

Yeshua once commented, "How blessed is anyone not offended by me"—literally, "How blessed is the one who is not scandalized by me" (Luke 7:23). Allow me to paraphrase his intent: "Blessed are the ones who are not embarrassed by my undignified, uncomfortable, untamed love. They are the ones who truly love me. They are the ones who will carry my love beyond human borders to people who are glutted with favors, yet starved for blessings. They are the ones who understand what it means to pray, 'Blessed be *Adonai* our God, king of the universe.'"

From the world's perspective, that's the love of a band of losers. From God's perspective, it's the only love worth giving one's life to attain.

A MEDITATION

Blessed be the Lord!
Blessed be the Servant-King!
Blessed be the Vulnerable God!

It's so easy to envision you as a regal ruler,
exalted upon your throne.
Or as a mighty warrior,
ready to fight for your people.
Or as the sovereign spirit,
turning nothingness into a living cosmos.

It's not so easy to envision you on your knees—
not exalted but on your knees—
on your knees
at my service,
at my disposal.

It's hard to accept the reality,
and the humility,
of a God
who chooses to be a blessing,
who chooses to be vulnerable.
And it's even harder to humble myself.
I don't mind bowing to some people . . .
kind people,
clean people,
righteous people.

But to bless anyone . . .
the unkind
(*Like it was my fault he was having a bad day!*),
the unclean
(*But, Lord, she hasn't taken a bath in months!*
And, well . . . I don't think her elevator stops on all the floors),
the unrighteous
(*OK, here's where I draw the line—*

It's his fault that he has AIDS
and I've got to think about my family's health.
No, I will not serve . . .
Yes, yes—I know . . . anyone).

Lord, why does it have to be so difficult?
I like to be selective in my service.
Let me serve like you served—
you weren't selective.
If you had been you would never have selected me.[14]

Unexpected Joy—
Embracing the Source of Delight

THE WEDDING BLESSINGS

Blessed be *Adonai* our God, king of the universe,
who created the fruit of the vine!

Blessed be *Adonai* our God, king of the universe,
who created everything for his glory!

Blessed be *Adonai* our God, king of the universe,
who created humanity!

Blessed be *Adonai* our God, king of the universe,
who created humanity in his image, creating them as
help-mates!

Blessed be *Adonai* our God, king of the universe,
who made the groom and bride to rejoice in each
other—may he give gladness to them as he gave
gladness to his creatures in the Garden of Eden!

Blessed be *Adonai* our God, king of the universe,
who created joy and happiness, bride and groom,
mirth, song, gladness and rejoicing, love and harmony,
peace and companionship!

Blessed be *Adonai* our God, king of the universe,
who causes the groom to rejoice in the bride!

Sheva B'rakhot
Jewish Wedding Blessings

The Roman Empire was as peaceful as it ever had been. Emperor Tiberius had ruled his father's sprawling domain for fifteen years. He was an able administrator who, according to the latest gossip, had a peculiar proclivity for prepubescent boys. The only urgent message on his desk concerned the collapse of a shoddily built theater in Fidenae. Nearly thirty thousand Romans had perished when the foundation suddenly failed.

The governor of the province of Judea—a new appointee named Pontius Pilate—had recently sent a squad of soldiers to the edge of the wilderness to check out a long-haired revolutionary who was prophesying about a new king. When they returned to Pilate's quarters, the soldiers were still guffawing. The self-proclaimed prophet smelled like a dead camel and looked worse. And he had the audacity to tell the soldiers to stop plundering people's property![1] How else could they make ends meet? Not on the paltry payments the Senate allotted them!

Few people in the provinces around the Sea of Galilee cared about Fidenae's building code or Pilate's soldiers or what happened in Tiberius's bedchambers on the isle of Capri. Most Galileans simply wanted every part of their lives to be left alone—especially their purses and their religious practices. Unfortunately, the Roman Empire meddled frequently in both. After a handful of skirmishes with Roman troops, the residents of Galilee became known as a gang of potential revolutionaries. The portrayal wasn't completely fair, but it stuck.

Herod Antipas, tetrarch of the Galilean province, had kept a lid on his provinces for three decades. While no one admired Antipas enough to extol him, no one despised him enough to dethrone him. That was probably as much as a professional politician could expect in Galilee. Of course, Antipas didn't strengthen his popularity among God-fearing people when he swapped his wife for a niece who also happened to be his sister-in-law. His standing in their polls took another nose-dive when he imported outsiders to populate the newly built port city of Tiberius.

But even the relentless shadows of the Roman Empire could not dim the joy that radiated from the Galilean village of Cana on this particular evening. The village of Cana was small—a scattered cluster of houses, draped across a terraced hill about 120 stadia west of Tiberius.[2] In the guestroom of one home, women and men reclined on woven mats and cushions. Embroidered tapestries spanned the chamber, forming tents above the friends and family members who had gathered in the bridegroom's newly built home. The mingled scents of smoldering lamps, human sweat, and spices soaked the sultry air.

The bride and her beloved stood before the *huppah*, the lavish canopy draped across one end of the room and the *heder*, the bed-chamber the couple would share when the wedding feast ended. The bride's hair, crowned with a circlet of ten silver coins and satu-rated with myrrh, glistened in the lamplight.[3] The bridegroom, shoulders encircled with a garland of flowers, declared, "She is my wife and I am her husband from this day and forever."[4] As the couple washed their hands in the stone water pots used for purifi-cation rites, the guests murmured, "Amen."

Natan'el Bar-Tolmai, one of the bridegroom's relatives, re-clined on a cushion beside the water pots.[5] He was a local boy— likable, but with a reputation for squandering his afternoons beneath the shade trees. His latest circle of friends reclined around him. Yet it wasn't Natan'el who had drawn this band together; the hub of the group was a young carpenter named Yeshua Bar-Yosef. He was a native of Nazareth, a seedy community about seventy-five stadia south of Cana.

The carpenter's mother lay behind her son. Drops of sweat wandered down her forehead, over the deep furrows and past the wisps of graying hair. Her eyes were fixed on the bride and her beloved, but her thoughts were far from Cana. She wondered if her eldest son would ever embrace a young woman before the *heder* and the *huppah*. If he did, what sort of woman would she be? He attracted the strangest mix of people. Natan'el and Philip were pious and polite. Shim'on, Andrew, and Zebedee's boys were rough but respectable. But then there was that tramp from Magdala! Miryam shuddered at the rumors she had heard about why the woman had suddenly left her village. Miryam wanted her son to be married—but not to a trollop like that, with red henna on her fingernails and galena[6] smeared around her eyes like plaster on the side of a stable! Why, oh *why*, Miryam wondered, does he let *her* hang around him? Who would end up at his side next?

Miryam knew why her son attracted such motley folk. It wasn't because he was the life of the party, although he delighted in feasts and enjoyed a good joke as much as anyone else. Nor was it his spontaneity, although he had been known to make friends by walking up to strangers and declaring, "Come after me!" Yeshua drew people to him because of the gentle strength that flowed from every word he spoke.

Her son's gentleness both captivated and terrified her. After thirty years, the words of the white-robed messenger still pierced her heart: "God will give him the throne of his forefather David; and he will rule the House of Ya'akov [Jacob] forever—there will be no end to his Kingdom!"[7] Had she heard the messenger's words correctly? Yeshua was the son of God—that she could never deny. Yet, if this mob that lounged around him comprised his army, how could he be the Messiah? And if his gentle wit was his only weapon, how could he become a king?

Miryam watched as the groom's father dipped a cup into the jar of wine. He raised the cup above the couple and spoke the *sheva b'rakhot*, the wedding blessings:

Blessed be *Adonai* our God, king of the universe,
   who created the fruit of the vine!

Blessed be *Adonai* our God, king of the universe,
   who created everything for his glory!

Blessed be *Adonai* our God, king of the universe,
   who created humanity!

Blessed be *Adonai* our God, king of the universe,
   who created humanity in his image, creating them as
   help-mates!

Blessed be *Adonai* our God, king of the universe,
   who made the groom and bride to rejoice in each
   other—may he give gladness to them as he gave
   gladness to his creatures in the Garden of Eden!

Blessed be *Adonai* our God, king of the universe,
   who created joy and happiness, bride and groom,
   mirth, song, gladness and rejoicing, love and harmony,
   peace and companionship!

Blessed be *Adonai* our God, king of the universe,
   who causes the groom to rejoice in the bride![8]

The newlyweds drained the cup, and raucous shouts erupted from Natan'el's circle of friends. The betrothal—that long season of waiting—was over. Now it was time for brimming cups of wine, yeasty chunks of bread, smoked slabs of lamb, and endless heaps of grapes and figs. The wedding feast had begun!

THE INFINITE EMPTINESS

From the beginning, every human heart has craved infinite delight. A dark hungry void gnaws at every human being's innermost self. "This infinite emptiness," Blaise Pascal declared, "can only be filled by an infinite and immutable object, that is to say, only by God himself."[9] Yet it is difficult to fathom this simple fact—that our thirst for infinite pleasure is, ultimately, a craving for the creator of pleasure. So, we try to quench our thirst with finite pleasures—another beer, another sexual partner, one more degree, one more dollar, a piece of fruit that promises the knowledge of good and evil. The personal compulsions differ, but the core problem remains the same: Few people truly believe that God is the source of pleasure. They cannot fathom that there are, in the psalmist's words, "unbounded joy" and "eternal delight" within the being of God (Ps. 16:11).

This simple fact is, however, clearly acknowledged in the wedding blessings that echoed in Yeshua's ears at the beginning of his earthly ministry. At every first-century Jewish wedding, the groom's father or a community leader repeated these words:

> Blessed be *Adonai* our God, king of the universe,
>   who made the groom and bride to rejoice in each
>   other—may he give gladness to them as he gave
>   gladness to his creatures in the Garden of Eden!
>
> Blessed be *Adonai* our God, king of the universe,
>   who created joy and happiness, bride and groom,
>   mirth, song, gladness and rejoicing, love and harmony,
>   peace and companionship!
>
> Blessed be *Adonai* our God, king of the universe,
>   who causes the groom to rejoice in the bride!

The wedding blessings explicitly acknowledge that the delight of the intimate relationship between a wife and her husband—perhaps the supreme expression of pleasure on the planet—is rooted in God. God is, from the perspective of the wedding blessings, the Source of Delight!

If God is "the Source of Delight," it shouldn't surprise us that one of the Hebrew prophets' favorite depictions of God's relationship with his people was the image of a passionate lover seeking the pleasure of his bride. [10] Here's how two of the prophets described God's relationship with his people:

> You developed, you reached puberty, your breasts appeared, and your hair grew long. . . . I passed by you, looked at you and saw that your time had come, the time for love. So I spread my cloak over you to cover your private parts and entered into a covenant with you, says *Adonai ELOHIM*, and you became mine. Then I bathed you in water, washed the blood off you, and anointed you with oil. I also clothed you with an embroidered gown, gave you fine leather sandals to wear, put a fine linen headband on your head and covered you with silk. . . . But now I am going to woo her—I will bring her out to the desert and I will speak to her heart. . . . She will respond there as she did when young, as she did when she came up from Egypt. (Ezekiel 16:7–10; Hosea 2:16–17)

God . . . depicted as a groom bathing with his bride and rejoicing in her nakedness? God . . . pictured as a husband, whisking away his wife to a secluded love nest where she responds like a newlywed for whom the experience is fresh and new? God . . . the Cosmic Lover, delighting in the pleasure of his people? God . . . the Source of Delight? Even though images of God as a passionate lover pervade the pages of Scripture, many aren't comfortable with such portrayals of God. In the view of some, pleasure may not be sinful, but it certainly isn't treated as sacred. Think about it: How often do couples kneel beside the bed before having sex and thank God for the feast that they are preparing to share? [11] How often do we recognize that every earthly pleasure has its ultimate source in God? Not nearly as often as we should, I suspect.

In essence, that's what is implied by the wedding blessings offered at weddings such as the one Yeshua attended in Cana. To embrace the implications of the wedding blessings is to admit that joy and pleasure are holy.

Of course, that doesn't mean that every *form* of joy or pleasure is holy. What it *does* mean is rejoicing in God's presence when I stroke my wife's skin and my heart begins to race . . . when I snuggle a toddler and savor the sweet scent of his hair . . . when I look at a sunset . . . when I am stuck in rush-hour traffic and take a few moments to think about the silvery sparkle of my daughter's giggle . . . when I recognize that God loves the one who constantly criticizes me and, therefore, I can love him too. To recognize God as the Source of Delight is to embrace every finite experience in my life as representation of God's infinite joy.

DIVINE PLEASURE VERSUS CULTURAL CONSUMERISM

If God truly is the Source of Delight, why do we have such a difficult time experiencing God in this way? One reason is that our culture has attempted to replace authentic pleasure and joy with *consumerism*. The gospel that consumerism proclaims to us is simple: *Consuming an excess of artificial pleasures can satisfy your hunger for infinite pleasure.* Television commercials and newspaper advertisements proclaim this gospel millions of times each day. According to one recent ad, "Whoever said it's better to give than to receive was obviously never on the receiving end of this car. . . . What more could you hope for?" Another ad declares, "This holiday, we'd like to encourage excessive drinking. Water, of course. . . . Indulge. It's a good thing."

The ditties may differ, but the results are the same: If we accept their message, life becomes a frenzied struggle for *more* as we try to fill our infinite emptiness with an excess of finite pleasures. The drunk tries to cure his hangover with another beer. The middle-aged man desperately combs the Internet for a more alluring picture of a more exquisite model in a more explicit pose. The first-grader wails in the aisle of Toys"R"Us, "If I only get this one, I'll never ask for another toy again!" The teen glances across the grandeur of the Painted Desert and declares with disgust, "We came all the way out here to see dirt, rocks, and dead trees?"—and then immerses himself in lifeless pixels prancing across the face of a handheld game. Adults have four-car garages attached to households of two, television sets in every room of the house, closets that bulge with clothes we never wear, and waistlines that bulge because of calories we never needed. In a consumerist culture:

> we no longer catch our breath at the sight of a rainbow or the scent of a rose, as we once did.... We no longer run our fingers through water, no longer shout at the stars, or make faces at the moon.... Certainly, the new can amaze us: a space shuttle, the latest computer game, the softest diaper. Till tomorrow, till the new becomes old, till yesterday's wonder is discarded or taken for granted.[12]

A few years ago, an article in *USA Today* included this unwitting indictment of consumerism:

> We buy, buy, buy, hoping to fill that empty, yearning hole in our soul. And as we rack up more debt, we buy possessions in a useless attempt to comfort ourselves. . . . Every time I add something to my pile, I feel a whoosh of pleasure, like a firework going off. And for a moment, everything's all right. But then, gradually, the light and sparkles disappear, and I'm left with cold, dark blackness again. So I look around feverishly for something else.... But the whooshes are getting shorter and shorter each time. Why won't the pleasure stay? Why don't I feel happier?[13]

The solution is not simply choosing to be satisfied with what we have—although that would be a good place to start! We must embrace the wisdom found in the ancient Jewish wedding blessings; we must authentically recognize God as the Source of Delight and allow him to satisfy our deepest longings. When we do, we begin to discover infinite joy in the ordinary events of our lives—in a glance or a touch or a song, in a field of corn or a friend who cares, in a moon or an amoeba, in a lifeless loaf that suddenly ~~symbolizes~~ the body of our Savior.[14]

WHAT DOES GOD DESIRE?

Unfortunately, our relationship with God frequently functions more like an impersonal business transaction than a passionate evening with one's spouse. Often, a high-pressure sales pitch brings someone down the aisle to sign a contract. Some congregations call the contract "An Application for Membership." Others use less formal clichés—"The Four Spiritual Laws" and "Admit, Believe, Confess." From the perspective of some people, these contracts grant Yeshua more or less complete control of their lives and require that they meet with him for occasional updates. In return, God grants them everlasting life.

Yet, no contract can compel what God desperately desires—passionate, joyous love. The central command of Scripture is "to love ADONAI your God with all your heart, all your being and all your resources (Deut. 6:5; see also Matt. 22:47 and Mark 12:30).

If I love my wife, I will not merely be faithful to her; I will delight in her with passion and joy. The author of the Proverbs explicitly ordered his son, "Let your fountain, the wife of your youth, be blessed. . . . let her breasts satisfy you at all times, always be infatuated with her love" (Prov. 5:18–19). Likewise, if I truly love God, I will passionately rejoice in him. One of Yeshua's followers wrote about his master, "Without having seen him, you love him. Without seeing him now, but trusting in him, you continue to be full of joy that is glorious beyond words" (1 Pet. 1:8). God's intent for humanity is infinite pleasure and joy.

WHEN GOD POPPED THE CORK

When we read the account of the wedding in Cana, it's easy to miss the point. Commentaries on the text offer plenty of facts and conjectures about first-century Jewish wedding feasts: Every guest brought gifts of food and wine. The feasts frequently lasted a full week. It was shameful if the food or wine ran out during the feast. Perhaps Miryam informed Yeshua that the wine was gone because he had not contributed anything to the feast. Perhaps God had revealed to Miryam that it was time for Yeshua to begin his earthly ministry. And perhaps, in the midst of these details and speculations, we miss the central point of the text: *In the person of Yeshua, the eternal pleasure of God erupted in the midst of the counterfeit pleasures of a fallen world.* His earthly ministry began at an event permeated with implications of pleasure. His first miracle was to transform the plain water of a cultural ritual into an exquisite drink of exhilaration and joy.[15] The earthly ministry of Yeshua began with these words ringing in his ears: "Blessed be *Adonai* our God, king of the universe, who made the groom and bride to rejoice in each other—may he give gladness to them as he gave gladness to his creatures in the Garden of Eden." How, then, can our relationship with God be anything less than a relationship rooted in infinite joy?

Let's put the point in more picturesque terms: In Yeshua, God popped the cork on the vintage wine he had stashed in his cellar at the dawn of time. Occasionally God had allowed the ancient prophets to sip this wine, but it was too strong for them. They ended up eating bugs for breakfast, choking down scrolls for dinner, dreaming about creatures with four faces, and bellowing about an unearthly burning in their bones (see Jer. 20:9; Ezek. 1:1–21; 3:1–3; Matt. 3:4). They could not manipulate the pleasure of God into a package that fit their agendas. The pleasure of God is like a magnum bottle of the finest Merlot—extravagant, unpredictable, overwhelming, and costly.

When God's people live the *sheva b'rakhot*—when they embrace God as the Source of Delight—nothing can remain the same. Waiting on others is no longer a chore—to serve others is to delight in our Beloved. The Lord's Supper is no longer a stale ritual in which a congregational leader fumbles with crumbled bits of crackers and thimble-sized cups of wine. It is a candlelight dinner with the love of our lives. The Scriptures are no longer a series of static principles that we always accept and occasionally obey. They are a precious love letter that gives us a glimpse of our Lover's deepest hopes and dreams.

Such an understanding of God transforms our prayers from a series of demands, aimed at making our lives easier, into an intimate conversation with our Beloved. Prayer becomes like slipping into a soothing tub of hot water and letting God's love wash over us and enfold us. Through prayer, we enter the inner chamber of our Beloved. He embraces us, and we explore each other with hunger and passion. We entwine our lives with the life of our Messiah, he enters the inmost part of our being, and we hear him gently whisper, "I'm wild about you."

LIVING IN ABANDONMENT

So, how do we embrace God as the Source of Delight? I wish that I could supply you with a seven-step plan, guaranteed to immerse your life in the joy of God. I can't. I'm still struggling to finish the first step (which is, I suspect, the only step—but it's a long, *long* step).

The first step is total abandonment to the desire to unite my life with the life of Yeshua, leaving behind all that binds me to lesser sources of delight. An ancient follower of Yeshua wrote, "Forgetting what is behind me and straining forward toward what lies ahead, I keep pursuing the goal in order to win the prize offered by God's upward calling" (Phil 3:13–14). This doesn't mean that we should abandon the pleasures of this life. Quite the opposite! When I abandon my life to Yeshua, every part of my life can *become* pleasurable because I embrace every moment as an opportunity to unite my life with the Source of Delight. In the words of one modern-day disciple,

> Jesus slept. I can unite my sleep with his. I'm having a rollicking good time at a Cajun barbecue in New Orleans. I shout with them, *"Laissez les bon temps rouler!"* Let the good times roll, and connect with Jesus who multiplied the wine at Cana to keep the party going. . . . Concretely, abandonment consists in seeing the will of God in all the people, events, and circumstances present to you. If God tears up our beautiful game plan and leads you into a valley instead of onto a mountaintop, it is because he wants you to discover *his* plan, which is more beautiful than anything you or I could have dreamed up.[16]

When I live in abandonment, I do not own my possessions. I recognize that I am only the temporary trustee of a tiny handful of God's possessions. That's why Yeshua commanded his followers, "When someone asks you for something, give it to him; when someone wants to borrow something from you, lend it to him. . . . if someone takes what belongs to you, don't demand it back" (Matt. 5:42; Luke 6:30). May I paraphrase his words? "Don't hesitate to let others use your belongings. If some of your possessions never find their way home, who cares? They belonged to God anyway. If God decides that he needs them back, he can find them without your help." That is living in abandonment.

To live in abandonment is to become *free*—free to give away anything that we possess; free to ignore the commercials that correlate our happiness with our buying habits; free to rejoice in the hints of our Redeemer's presence in every part or our lives; free to gaze into the heavens, to feel the gentle caress of God, and to sing into the wind, "I am so joyful in ADONAI! My soul rejoices in my God, for he has clothed me in salvation, dressed me with a robe of triumph, like a bridegroom wearing a festive turban, like a bride adorned with her jewels" (Isa. 61:10). Only then have we experienced authentic joy. Only then can we be satisfied. For only then have we embraced the sweeping implications of the simple prayer, "Blessed be *Adonai* our God, king of the universe, who created joy and happiness."

A MEDITATION

My Lord, my Lover, the Source of my Joy,
Let me rejoice in you.
Let me delight in your creation,
in sun and surf,
in snow and star,
in blue marlin and robin redbreast,
in the people that I love to love
in the people that I would prefer not to love,
in the pleasure of your presence within me.
Let me live a life of abandonment—
a life in which I let go of everything,
everything that shackles me to yesterday,
everything that imprisons me in my small self today,
everything that terrifies me with the uncertainty of tomorrow,
everything except you.
Let me find my pleasure in you—
because then (and only then) am I free.
Please, let me be free.[17]

Knowing the God Whose
Gifts Go Beyond Our Expectations

The followers of Yeshua expected the king of Israel—
what they got was a Messiah who
refused to be limited by human borders.
The followers of Yeshua expected to become royal
    warriors—
Yeshua told them to become the children
of his Father instead.
The followers of Yeshua expected their friend Lazarus
to erupt from his tomb at the end of time—
four days after he died,
they ate dinner with him.
In the end, the folks who tagged along with Yeshua
received nothing they expected,
very little they wanted,
and everything they needed.
Still today,
that tends to be the way
God answers prayer.

When Prayer Becomes Perilious— Receiving the Gift of God's Presence

PRAYERS IN THE SYNAGOGUE OF NAZARETH

Accept your people, *Adonai* our God, and receive their prayer. Restore the most holy service of your house and accept in love the offerings and prayers of Israel. May it please you always to want to accept the service of Your people Israel. May our eyes see you return to Zion in mercy. Blessed be *Adonai*, who restores his presence to Zion.

> *Avodah* (Service)
> Seventeenth *B'rakhah* of the *Amidah*

Blessed be *Adonai*, the ruler of the world. You formed light, and you created darkness. You formed peace, and you created all things. In your mercy, you give light to the earth and to everyone who lives on the earth. In your goodness, you renew your creation daily. Blessed be *Adonai* our God for the glory of his works! Blessed be *Adonai* our God for the lights, which he made for his praise! Blessed be *Adonai* our God, who formed light!

> Invocation for the Synagogue Service

Yeshua returned to the Galil [Galilee] in the power of the Spirit, and reports about him spread throughout the countryside. He taught in their synagogues, and everyone respected him. Now when he went to Natzeret [Nazareth], where he had been brought up, on *Shabbat* he went to the synagogue as usual. He stood up to read, and he was given the scroll of the prophet Yesha'yahu [Isaiah]. Unrolling the scroll, he found the place where it was written:

> The Spirit of ADONAI is upon me;
> therefore he has anointed me
> to announce Good News to the poor;

he has sent me to proclaim freedom for the imprisoned
and renewed sight for the blind,
to release those who have been crushed,
to proclaim a year of the favor of ADONAI.

After closing the scroll and returning it to the *shammash*
[attendant], he sat down; and the eyes of everyone in the
synagogue were fixed on him. He started to speak to them:
"Today, as you heard it read, this passage of the *Tanakh*
[Hebrew Scriptures] was fulfilled!" Everyone was speaking
well of him and marvelling that such appealing words were
coming from his mouth. (Luke 4:14–22a)

The double-blast of the ram's horn echoed again over the Galilean mountains before slipping southward, across the Plain of Esdraelon. The sun, setting on the other side of Mount Carmel, cast a shadow across the cluster of buildings nestled in the breast of Mount Tabor. On the flat roof of one house, the *shammash* laid aside his trumpet and watched the residents of Nazareth scurry toward the synagogue. This *Shabbat*, the synagogue would be full. Yeshua had returned home—and everyone hoped to see a miracle.

The residents of Nazareth were not excited because they loved the son of Yosef—far from it; most of them had ignored him when he lived among them. They were excited because the crowds from Cana and Capernaum had claimed that Yeshua could heal the sick, that he spoke like a prophet, that his teachings were plain and yet powerful. At first, they had scoffed and snorted—*Yeshua Bar-Yosef, a prophet? Ha! A donkey would be more likely to proclaim God's message than Yosef's son!* Still, the tidings continued. *He's a prophet . . . a healer . . . perhaps the Messiah!* Now, Yeshua Bar-Yosef had returned to his hometown. This *Shabbat*, he would serve as the *shaliakh tzibbur* (teacher of the congregation) in the synagogue of Nazareth—and everyone hoped to see a miracle.

Within the synagogue, a circle of candles chased away the darkness around the *Aron Hakodesh* (holy ark)—the chest where the sacred scrolls rested, wrapped in linen. The leaders of the synagogue sat in the seats of honor[1] beside the *Aron Hakodesh*. As the citizens of Nazareth slipped into the synagogue, they glanced eagerly at the seats of honor . . . but Yeshua was not there. Their eyes desperately scanned the congregation. *Where is . . . has he . . . there . . . among the common people . . . silent . . . head covered and bowed . . . Yeshua of Nazareth.*

At last, the *shammash* stood and summoned Yeshua. Strained silence swept the congregation as Yeshua ascended the platform and stood behind the lectern. A firm voice filled the room with an invocation:

> Blessed be *Adonai*, the ruler of the world. You formed light, and you created darkness. You formed peace, and you created all things. In your mercy, you give light to the earth and to everyone who lives on the earth. In your goodness, you renew your creation daily. Blessed be *Adonai* our God for the glory of his works! Blessed be

Adonai our God for the lights, which he made for his praise! Blessed be *Adonai* our God, who formed light!

You have loved us with great love, *Adonai* our God. You have comforted us with overflowing compassion, our Father and our King. Have mercy on us and teach us, for the sake of our ancestors who trusted in you and who received from you the laws of life. Open our eyes to your law. Cause our hearts to cling to your commandments. Unite our hearts to love and fear your name. Then, we shall never be put to shame. For you are a God who creates salvation! You have chosen us from among all nations and languages! Truly, you have drawn us close to your name—*Selah*—so that we can lovingly praise you in your Oneness. Blessed be *Adonai*, who lovingly chose Israel as his people![2]

Yeshua recited the *Sh'ma*, then turned toward the *Aron Hakodesh* and knelt. The congregation joined him as he began to repeat the *Amidah*. As he recited the last few blessings of the familiar prayer, the crowd began to grow restless, anticipating what miracle Yeshua might perform in their midst.

Accept your people, *Adonai* our God, and receive their prayer. May it please you always to want to accept the service of your people Israel. May our eyes see you return to Zion in mercy. Blessed be *Adonai*, who restores His Presence to Zion.

We thank you, for it is you alone who is *Adonai* our God and the God of our fathers, forever and ever. You are the Rock and Shield of our salvation, you alone, from generation to generation. We thank you and tell of your praise, for our lives are in your hands and our souls are trusting in you. Every day your miracles are with us: Your wonders and favors are at all times, evening, morning, and afternoon. You who are good, your compassions are never exhausted and your kindnesses are continual. We put our hope in you.

For all these things we bless and exalt your Name, our king forever and evermore. And all the living shall confess you forever and praise your Name in truth, God of our salvation and our help forever! Blessed are you, *Adonai*, your Name is good, and to you it is right to give thanks.[3]

After removing the *Torah* scroll from the *Aron Hakodesh*, the *shammash* unwound the blue and crimson cloths, ascended the platform, and unrolled the sacred scroll. The first leader of the synagogue read a portion from the Law of Moses, then the second, and the third. With each reading, the anticipation intensified. After the *Torah* readings, Yeshua would begin to teach—and everyone hoped to see a miracle. Finally, after the seventh reading, the *shammash* nodded to Yeshua.

Yeshua accepted the scroll of the prophet Isaiah and ascended the platform. The only sound in the synagogue was a faint rustling as Yeshua unrolled the scroll and deliberately skimmed the columns of sacred text. Suddenly, he stopped and surveyed the congregation . . . the women, clustered together near the back of the gathering-place . . . the men and older boys, jammed into the same narrow, wooden benches where Yeshua had sat in the years following his *bar mitzvah* . . . late arrivals, standing in the dim corners, barely visible amid the flickering candles . . . a few people outside, peering through the windows. At last, he began to read, speaking as if he knew the words by heart, paraphrasing the Hebrew text into Aramaic:

The Spirit of ADONAI is upon me;
therefore he has anointed me
to announce Good News to the poor;
he has sent me to proclaim freedom for the imprisoned
and renewed sight for the blind,
to release those who have been crushed,
to proclaim a year of the favor of ADONAI.[4]

Yeshua waited as the congregation absorbed the final echoes of the prophecy. He handed the scroll to the *shammash* and lowered himself into the chair beside the lectern. Few people could escape the irony—a carpenter's son, sitting in the seat of the teacher. Yeshua leaned forward, squinting slightly in the fading light. His eyes seemed to pierce each person's deepest plans and plumb their darkest secrets. He paused for a moment and savored the familiar scents of the synagogue, the curious mixture of candle-wax and leather scrolls, fragrant oils and human sweat. When Yeshua spoke, he spoke with absolute certainty and authority: "Today, as you heard it read, this passage of the *Tanakh* was fulfilled!"

THE PERIL OF PRAYER

Prayer is perilous. It's dangerous. It's utterly unsafe. In fact, if prayer were a substance, the Surgeon General would probably slap a warning label on it. And why not? Moses asked God for mercy and spent the next four decades coddling God's people across the desert. Elijah prayed for fire and found himself on the queen's list of most-wanted criminals. The prophet Isaiah cried, "I'm here, send me!" and—according to tradition—his king sawed him in half. Yeshua prayed, "Not what I want, but what you want"—and spent six hours on an execution stake. Get the picture? Prayer is hazardous to personal comfort and safety.

Several dozen Galileans discovered the danger of prayer one summer afternoon in Nazareth. They entreated their God, "May our eyes see you return to Zion in mercy." What was so risky about this snippet from the synagogue liturgy? The people had repeated this blessing every *Shabbat* since their childhood. The danger was that, *this* time, God answered their prayer, and God's answer defied their definitions of "Zion."

In the synagogue blessing, "Zion" didn't refer only to the craggy hill where Solomon constructed the Temple—although the return of God's presence to the Temple mount was certainly implied. Here, "Zion" also pointed to the people of God. This connotation was as ancient as the prophets: God himself had once declared, "Tziyon [Zion] says, 'ADONAI has abandoned me, ADONAI has forgotten me. . . .' But I have engraved you on the palms of my hands, your walls are always before me" (Isa. 49:14–22). The author of Hebrews echoed this understanding of Zion when he wrote, "You have come to Mount Tziyon, . . . to a community of the firstborn whose names have been recorded in heaven" (Heb. 12:22–23).

This much, the residents of Nazareth understood. When they said, "Return to Zion in mercy," they were asking God to live in peace among his people. They could even handle the idea that Yeshua was God's chosen representative. When Yeshua said, "Today, as you heard it read, this passage of the *Tanakh* was fulfilled," they didn't balk. In fact, "everyone was speaking well of him and marveling that such appealing words were coming from his mouth" (Luke 4:22). Sure, they expressed some doubt. Yet they remained willing to listen—and, perhaps, to wait for a miracle. Then came the clincher: God's works of wonder were available to *anyone* who would submit to God's ways—*even Gentiles.*

> "It's true, I'm telling you—when Eliyahu was in Isra'el, and the sky was sealed off for three-and-a-half years, so that all the Land suffered severe famine, there were many widows; but Eliyahu was sent to none of them, only to a widow in Tzarfat [Zarephath] in the land of Tzidon [Sidon]. Also there were many people with *tzara'at* in Isra'el during the time of the prophet Elisha; but not one of them was healed, only Na'aman the Syrian." On hearing this, everyone in the synagogue was filled with fury. (Luke 4:25–28)

Na'aman the Syrian and the widow of Zarephath in Sidon had one thing in common: Neither one was Jewish. The congregation had prayed, "Return to Zion in mercy," and God had answered their prayer. In the words of Yochanan, "The Word became a human being and lived with us"—literally, "pitched a tent among us" (John 1:14). Yet God pitched his tent on his own terms and in his own way. And it was difficult for the residents of Nazareth to grasp how God could drive his tent-stakes beyond them. The hometown boy's words shattered the demographics that drove their congregational growth strategy. "Zion" might encompass the poor, the blind, the imprisoned, and the oppressed. But Syrians and Sidonians? That was more difficult. Yet, according to the carpenter's son, God's target audience included *all* sorts of people.

Starving widows and Syrian army officers.
Roman centurions and sticky-fingered tax collectors.
Pious hypocrites and down-and-out prostitutes.

People who cart thirty-seven items through the express lane.
The neighbor whose dog gets on your nerves.
The driver who cuts you off on the exit ramp.
All sorts of people.

THE HARDEST PART OF PRAYER

The hardest part of prayer is neither learning to pray nor receiving
an answer to our prayers. The most difficult part of prayer is
recognizing and accepting the answers when they come. God's
answers often challenge our assumptions; simply put, God's answers
often cost us more than we are willing to pay. Why? Because
authentic prayers are unsafe—just like the One to whom we pray.
Consider this scene from *The Lion, the Witch, and the Wardrobe*:

> "If there's anyone who can appear before Aslan without
> their knees knocking, they're either braver than most or
> just silly," said Mrs. Beaver.
> "Then he isn't safe?" said Lucy.
> "Safe?" said Mr. Beaver. "Don't you hear what Mrs.
> Beaver tells you? Who said anything about safe? 'Course
> he isn't safe. But he's good. He's the King, I tell you." [5]

God, like his answers to our prayers, is never safe, but he's
always good. But let's be honest: Most of us would rather avoid
answers that defy our expectations. In fact, the vast majority of
human beings would prefer that God leave them alone until they
need him to fulfill their desires. In Elie Wiesel's novel, *Twilight*, God
laments, "All these creatures that breathe because of me, what do
they want? That I keep quiet, that I keep out of their lives. But
when I remain silent, they reproach me. When I speak, they call me
arbitrary."[6] If we are honest, none of us wants God to challenge our
expectations. No one longs for unsafe answers to prayer. Not you.
Not me. *No one.*

So, we protect ourselves in one of two ways: We pray prayers
that are unsafe but insincere, or we pray prayers that are safe but
petty. In the first case, our prayers are a lie; in the second case,
our prayers are empty. In both cases, we miss the grandeur of
God's plan.

UNSAFE BUT INSINCERE—PRAYER AS MEANINGLESS RITUAL

Sports are so merciful. In baseball, you return to the dugout after three strikes. In basketball, you commit five fouls, and you get to warm the bench. Oh, I know, sitting on the bench doesn't feel merciful at the time. But who wants to fail to connect with the ball eighteen consecutive times? Or double-dribble the twenty-fourth time? The rules spare players the pain of persistent failure. If only life were as merciful as sports. If only we could sit on the bench after two fast balls and an unexpected curve ball.

I recall a week when life sent me more than my share of curve balls. I was struggling to balance my seminary studies with my responsibilities as the pastor of a small congregation. Our aging Ford Escort had stripped a timing belt. I had failed to finish an important assignment because of our car problems. When Rayann and I arrived home on Friday evening, an insufficient funds notice greeted us from our mailbox. When we sat down to eat dinner, I was disheartened, discouraged, depressed—everything except prayerful. Yet, a curious combination of custom and commitment compelled me to say a blessing. I drew a deep breath and recited the familiar cliché, "Lord, I thank you for this day and for . . ." I stopped. *What am I thinking? Thank God for this day? I'm not thankful for today. In fact, I wish I could have skipped this entire week! How can I be thankful for stalled cars, stingy congregational committees, and short checking balances? I don't even want to be thankful!* I had prayed pious words, but I hadn't meant a single word that I said. The dilemma isn't confined to dinner tables at the end of no-good-awful-rotten days.

Consider a petition you may have heard recently: "Your Kingdom come"—but, of course, we want the soundtrack for the coming of the Kingdom and the carpet in his palace to suit our personal tastes. Another common prayer: "Let your will be done"—but heaven forbid that God's will might require me to embrace that person who chafes my nerves. Such prayers are pious, perilous, unsafe . . . and utterly insincere.

What we fail to recognize, though, is that, whenever God defies our expectations, it is because he longs to give us something greater than our expectations. When I resist unexpected answers to my prayers, I am like a child born in 1895 whose father promised him a horse for his twenty-first birthday. Suppose that, in 1916, the son received a Model-T Ford instead. "It would be a strange son who would accuse his father of breaking his promise just because there was no horse. . . . It is obvious that . . . the father has more than kept his promise. In fact he has done so in a way that *surpasses* the original words of the promise."⁷ That's how God answers our prayers. Whenever God's answer *defies* our expectation, it also *surpasses* our expectation. Yet, how do we respond? Look again at the people that had asked God, "Return to Zion in mercy": "On hearing this, everyone in the synagogue was filled with fury. They rose up, drove him out of town, and dragged him to the edge of the cliff on which their town was built, intending to throw him off" (Luke 4:28–29).

When our prayers are unsafe but insincere, we would rather shove God off the edge of a cliff than lay our greed and self-indulgence at his feet. We would rather grovel and grope after our own barren fantasies than embrace the reality of a God who will give us his best—but only if we will leave the choice to him.

SINCERE BUT PETTY—PRAYER AS PERSONAL PACIFIER

There is another way to avoid unsafe answers to our prayers: Praying in ways that are sincere but petty. When people gather for prayer, their requests may include such items as, "I really need to pass a test tomorrow." "Keep my friends safe as they travel." "My brother-in-law's cousin's aunt has an ingrown toenail." I'm not saying that any of these requests is wrong: God *does* care about science tests, safe travels, and smarting toenails. Yet, when our times of prayer focus primarily on human needs, we are settling for less than what God intended. Prayer becomes, like an infant's pacifier, a gadget that brings fleeting gratification but fails to give us what we need to be able to grow. We forget that the primary purpose of prayer is not to receive blessings for ourselves. The purpose of prayer is to receive and to rejoice in God himself.

We are like the tourist who traveled to Switzerland, wanting to meet one of the foremost theologians of the twentieth century, Karl Barth. The tourist boarded a bus and unwittingly seated himself beside Barth. "What do you want to see in our city?" Barth asked the man. He replied, "I would like to see the great theologian, Karl Barth. Do you know him?" "Oh yes," said Barth, "I shave him every morning."⁸ The tourist left the bus ecstatic, telling his friends that he had met Barth's barber, when he could have enjoyed an encounter with Barth himself. "We are," C. S. Lewis wrote, "half-hearted creatures, fooling about with drink and sex and ambition when infinite joy is offered us, like an ignorant child who wants to go on making mud pies in a slum because he cannot imagine what is meant by the offer of a holiday at the sea. We are far too easily pleased."⁹

Why do we satisfy ourselves with anything less than an encounter with the living God? Because petty prayers are comfortable, familiar, and painless—everything that an encounter with the living God *isn't*. Suppose that we sincerely and passionately prayed, "God, return to Zion! Do whatever it takes to reveal yourself among your people." What might happen? Think about a few times that God actually answered that prayer: God revealed himself to Moses on the mountain, and the people screamed, "Don't let God speak with us, or we will die!" (Exod. 20:19). God revealed himself in Yeshua, and all humanity shrieked in unison, "Put him to death on the stake!" (Mark 15:13). God revealed himself to the followers of Yeshua on *Shavu'ot* (Pentecost), and, within five chapters, the preachers found themselves in prison, a deacon ended up dead, and two principal donors to their congregation's benevolent fund left the pastor's office on stretchers (Acts 2–8). Is it any wonder that we settle for petty prayers? Authentic prayer costs us deeply because it brings us into the presence of the one who declared, "If anyone wants to come after me, let him say 'No' to himself, take up his execution-stake, and keep following me" (Mark 8:34).

Yeshua once asked, "Is there any father here who, if his son asked him for a fish, would instead of a fish give him a snake? or if he asked for an egg would give him a scorpion? So if you, even though you are bad, know how to give your children gifts that are good, how much more will the Father keep giving the *Ruach HaKodesh* from heaven to those who keep asking him!" (Luke 11:11–13). Yes, it's true: God always gives his children fish instead of snakes and eggs instead of scorpions, and he grants his Spirit to us to prove his good intentions. But the fish may not always be prepared in the way that we expected and, sometimes, the eggs are not to our liking. Yet, amid the fish, eggs, and shattered ex- pectations, God offers us the greatest gift of all: "The God you call upon with even your most half-cocked and halting prayer will finally come down the path you beat, and even if he does not bring the answer you want, he will bring you himself."[10] Then, the question confronts us again: Will we embrace him as our Master, regardless of the cost? Or, will we tread the well-worn trail that leads to the edge of the cliff? It depends on whether we want to say honestly, "Return to Zion."

A MEDITATION

Oh Lord, my God,
the Highest God,
the Creator of heaven and earth,
my Shield and the Shield of my ancestors—
It's easy to ask you to return in mercy to Zion.
It's tough to ask you to return in mercy to me.
But there are so many dirty corners,
so many dark crannies,
so many prejudices and preconceptions
that only you can see.
Do I really want you to return to my life—even if it hurts?
Do I really want you to transform me—whatever the cost?
Do I really want *you?*
I hope so.
Yet, I need so much more than hope.
I need help.
I need *you.*

When the Kingdom Isn't Where You Expected It to Be—Receiving the Gift of God's Reign

THE PRAYER OF THE *TALMIDIM* (DISCIPLES) AND PARALLEL JEWISH PRAYERS

You, therefore, pray like this: "Our Father in heaven! May your Name be kept holy. May your Kingdom come, your will be done on earth as in heaven. Give us the food we need today. Forgive us what we have done wrong, as we too have forgiven those who have wronged us. And do not lead us into hard testing, but keep us safe from the Evil One. For kingship, power and glory are yours forever." (Matt. 6:9–13)

Magnified and sanctified be His great name in the world which He created according to His will. And may He establish his kingdom during your life and during your days, and during the life of all the house of Israel, speedily and in the near future.... Blessed, praised and glorified, exalted, extolled and honored, adored and lauded be the Name of the Holy One, blessed be He, beyond all blessings and hymns, praises and songs that are uttered in the world.

From the *Kaddish*[1]

Our God and the God of our fathers, ... remove our guilt and blot out our iniquities, as you have promised. ... Blessed be *Adonai*, who forgives transgressions, the king of the universe, the one who sanctifies Israel and the Day of Atonement.[2]

Yom Kippur (Day of Atonement) Prayer

Lead me not into sin, or into iniquity, or into temptation. And may the good inclination have sway over me and let not the evil inclination have sway over me.[3]

Rabbinic Prayer

The big fisherman stopped for a moment when he reached the crest of the hill. He brushed an unruly black curl away from his eyes and glanced down the hillside. Heavy spring rains had washed over Galilee again, leaving sandy gouges in the slopes. The village of Capernaum meandered crookedly along the bottom of the hill. Smoke wandered upward from courtyards and rooftops and mingled with the morning fog to form a luminous haze in the sunlight.

Beyond the clusters of black basalt houses, the Sea of Galilee stretched southward, toward Samaria. The rising sun was already chasing away the silken wisps of fog that remained on the lake.[4] A half-dozen boats darted through the fading mist, toward the docks that dotted the rocky shore. Burly fishermen, bare chested and sun-bronzed, stood in the bows, bellowing good-natured curses and grudging compliments at their competitors. Another night of fishing had ended. Now, the race was on. Merchants were already flocking to the docks, prepared to trade fistfuls of gleaming *denarii* for the slender barbels and stubby perches that writhed beneath the decks of the boats.

It was all so familiar to Shim'on. The pungent scents of fresh fish and lake water, the thrill of hauling a net, gorged with fish, into the boat. So many years of mending nets and patching leaks, so many stormy nights, so many frantic dashes to the shore . . . and now—what? He glimpsed his barren boat and his nets, decaying along the shore. Not for the first time, a deluge of doubt chilled his stomach.

At first, it had been an adventure—rambling across the Galilean hills alongside the carpenter-turned-rabbi. Yeshua's claims were radical, revolutionary, maybe even messianic. Then, a few simpletons claimed that the rabbi from Nazareth had healed them. Suddenly the little flock of learners had erupted into a horde of crackpots and cripples, hustlers and whores.[5]

Now, when Yeshua spent the night in Shim'on's home in Capernaum,[6] the only person who rejoiced was the local tavern-keeper. After glutting themselves with wine, the swarm of ragamuffins slept in the streets around Shim'on's house—and did who-knows-what in the shadowed alleys. Shim'on had become the laughingstock of his hometown. His friends accused him of catching "Messiah fever." His father had publicly labeled him a fool.

The moneybag that dangled from his belt was limp. What else could it possibly cost him to follow this rabbi?

"Shim'on! Shim'on Bar-Yochanan!"

It was Andrew. Shim'on turned and pinpointed his younger brother at the center of the crowd, near the teacher's side. A few wealthy merchants were selling their wares from the tents that they had pitched along the edges of the mob. The rest of the rabble sprawled in the sun, laughing and frolicking. The big fisherman ambled past the tents and arrived at Andrew's side just in time to see his rabbi let a scrawny waif wrestle him to the ground. Yeshua emerged from a cluster of toddlers and leaped to his feet, laughing. Without warning, he lifted his hands. The crowd turned silent.

Shim'on sat on the ground between two of his former fishing partners. The teacher wandered among the people, embracing them one by one, whispering blessings to the children. Finally, he returned to the center of the crowd. He squatted beside Shim'on and stared into his eyes. Shim'on squirmed and longed for a place to hide. Yet, he sensed that no rock in all of Galilee could possibly shield him from Yeshua's gaze. Somehow, Yeshua seemed to sense every uncertainty, each misgiving, in Shim'on's heart. Yeshua gripped the fisherman's bulky shoulder.

"Shim'on, are you poor?"

Yeshua spoke gently, but every person in the crowd heard him clearly. Shim'on nodded sheepishly and tossed the rabbi his empty moneybag. Yeshua kissed Shim'on and hurled the goatskin bag into the air.

"How blessed are you poor![7] for the Kingdom of God is yours."

Laughter erupted throughout the crowd. Then, a few folks glimpsed the seriousness in the teacher's eyes. Laughter faded into dumbstruck silence. Yeshua wasn't joking.

He ruffled a grubby urchin's hair and asked, "Are you hungry?"

The boy nodded vigorously. The rabbi seized the child in his arms and whirled toward the crowd:

> How blessed are you who are hungry!
> for you will be filled.
> How blessed are you who are crying now!
> for you will laugh.
> How blessed you are whenever people hate you and

ostracize you and insult you and denounce you as a
criminal on account of the Son of Man.
Be glad when that happens; yes, dance for joy!
because in heaven your reward is great.
For that is just how their fathers treated the prophets.

Yeshua released the boy and pointed to the tents at the edge of the
crowd.

But woe to you who are rich,
for you have already had all the comfort you will get!
Woe to you who are full now,
for you will go hungry!
Woe to you who are laughing now,
for you will mourn and cry!
Woe to you when people speak well of you,
for that is just how their fathers treated the false
prophets!
Nevertheless, to you who are listening, what I say is
this: "Love your enemies! Do good to those who hate
you, bless those who curse you, pray for those who
mistreat you."

Yeshua scrambled up the side of a massive rock and sat atop the
stone. Silhouetted against the sapphire sky, his tan tunic snapping
in the wind, he began to teach. His words rang across the hills like
the blasts of a *shofar*:

When you pray, don't be like the hypocrites, who love
to pray standing in the synagogues and on street
corners, so that people can see them. Yes! I tell you, they
have their reward already! But you, when you pray, go
into your room, close the door, and pray to your
Father in secret. Your Father, who sees what is done in
secret, will reward you. And when you pray, don't
babble on and on like the pagans, who think God will
hear them better if they talk a lot. Don't be like them,
because your Father knows what you need before you
ask him.

You, therefore, pray like this . . .

Yeshua turned his face upward and stretched out his hands, smiling as he spoke,

> Our Father in heaven! May your Name be kept holy. May your Kingdom come, your will be done on earth as in heaven. Give us the food we need today. Forgive us what we have done wrong, as we too have forgiven those who have wronged us. And do not lead us into hard testing, but keep us safe from the Evil One.[8]

Shim'on exhaled slowly. How long had he been holding his breath? He couldn't remember. "Your Kingdom come," the carpenter had said. *But when?* Shim'on wondered, *and how? There are only twelve of us that he's called to be his followers—and I was the only one who had enough sense to bring my sword!* "Your Kingdom come?" *Not with this motley mess of people, and not with a leader who spends his time wrestling with children instead of sharpening his sword!* "Kingdom come?" *That's what he said, but what I've seen so far isn't like any Kingdom I've ever seen before.*

The big fisherman glanced down the slopes again, his eyes gently tracing his boat's familiar bow. Was it worth the cost to traipse along the hills behind this teacher from Nazareth? Was there really a Kingdom coming? Or were his father and friends right after all? At this point, Shim'on Bar-Yochanan wasn't sure.

WHERE IS "YOUR KINGDOM COME?"

Ever since humanity's failure in the Garden of Eden, people have been longing for a larger world, a kingdom unseen. Each of their journeys tends to begin in the same way—an unexplainable restlessness, a longing for an unknown circumstance to which a divine voice seemed to be calling them, a yearning for a place of perfect peace and love. Before Yeshua's followers could ask where or why, they were headed for a distant land where they believed that their dreams would come true.

The destinations may differ, but the dream remains the same. It's the longing expressed in the Prayer of the *Talmidim*: "Your

Kingdom come . . . on earth." In other words, "Let us find a place on earth where your presence is as evident as it is in the heavens." Abram was one ancient victim of this longing. Abram's father, Terah, had sensed the restlessness first. One day, he unexpectedly piled his belongings and his children on the humps of his prize camels and headed out from Ur to Haran—the ancient equivalent of a trip from Philadelphia to Phoenix. When they reached Haran, Terah's energy and his family's patience were all but spent. So, Terah settled down in Haran long enough to die there.

Maybe Abram and Sarai tried to settle down too. Maybe they laid a foundation beneath their tent, planted some shrubbery around the entrance, joined a civic club. If so, it didn't last. Before long, Sarai found Abram out behind the tent, sitting on his camel, staring into the sunset. She recognized that restless look in his eyes. It was the look that said that, no matter where they were, they weren't *there* yet. It was the look that said he could see "your Kingdom come," but only in the distance, just past the horizon.[9]

Finally, God told Abram that it was time to load up the camels again: "Get yourself out of your country, away from your kinsmen and away from your father's house, and go to the land that I will show you" (Gen. 12:1). According to the author of Hebrews, "He was looking forward to a city with permanent foundations, of which the architect and builder is God. . . . All these people . . . aspire to a better fatherland, a heavenly one" (Heb. 11:10, 13, 16). In other words, they were searching for "Kingdom come."

The problem was that neither Abraham nor his descendants were certain where they could find God's Kingdom or even what it was. So they wandered form Haran to Canaan, from Canaan to Egypt, across the Sinai Peninsula, into the Promised Land, then to the rivers of Babylon and back again. It's no wonder that the first words the Hebrews spoke when they entered their land were, "My father was a nomad from Aram" (see Deut. 26:1–11). Restlessness was in their blood.

By the time John began immersing along Jordan's banks, most Israelites weren't traveling anymore. Yet they were still waiting, yearning, aching, for the city that is "to come" (Heb. 13:14). Every first-century Jew, including Yeshua and his followers, expressed this longing during the synagogue service: "May He establish his kingdom during your life and during your days, and during the life of all the house of Israel, speedily and in the near future." In other words, "Your Kingdom come."

WHAT MAKES THE PRAYER OF THE *TALMIDIM* DIFFERENT?

Given this longing, it isn't surprising that the Disciples' Prayer includes a plea for the coming of God's Kingdom. In fact, most of the expressions found in this prayer were at least vaguely familiar to Yeshua's first followers. On Yom Kippur, faithful Jews prayed, "Pardon our transgressions." In times of temptation, they whispered, "Lead me not into sin, or into iniquity, or into temptation." The *Kaddish*—a prayer spoken in every synagogue service as well as in times of mourning—asked for the sanctification of God's name ("sanctified be His name in the world") and the coming of God's kingdom ("may He establish his kingdom").

The holiness of God's name, the coming of God's kingdom, the plea for deliverance from temptation—all of them were familiar concepts to Yeshua and his followers. What, then, is unique about the Disciples' Prayer?

First, it's the *location* of God's kingdom. What Abraham, the children of Israel, and the first followers of Yeshua had such difficulty grasping was the fact that they were not hungering for a kingdom they could plow or build or own. Yeshua made the matter clear to a handful of religious leaders when he said, "The Kingdom of God . . . does not come with visible signs; nor will people be able to say, 'Look! Here it is!' or, 'Over there!' Because, you see, the Kingdom of God is among you" (Luke 17:20–21). The Kingdom that you have craved so long is *among you*—among you in the flesh of the carpenter from Nazareth (see also John 10:38; 14:6–11, 20). The kingdom is *among you*, for the kingdom is the place where Yeshua is present.

Ancient kings might declare, in moments of passion, "Whatever your request, up to half the kingdom, it will be given to you" (Esther 5:3). Through the Prayer of the *Talmidim*, the king of all creation declares to his children, "Ask me anything you wish. You can never ask for more than I have already given to you. For my presence *is* my kingdom, and through Yeshua my Son, that is precisely what I have already given to you."

The second aspect of the Prayer of the *Talmidim* that makes it unique is the *means* by which God's Kingdom comes. "Our Father," the prayer begins, informing us from the outset that, if we are to experience this Kingdom, it will be by recognizing our role as *children of our heavenly Father.* "Unless you change and become like little children," Yeshua once commented to the people around him, "you won't even enter the Kingdom of Heaven!" (Matt. 18:3). Another time, he laughed, looked toward the sky, and said, "Father, Lord of heaven and earth, I thank you because you concealed these things from the sophisticated and educated, yet revealed them to ordinary people"—literally, "to little children" (Luke 10:21).

So, what does it mean to pray as a child? In the first-century world to be a child was not to be naïve or to possess "childlike faith." To be a child was *to have no rights.*

> In the present day, we tend to idealize childhood as the happy age of innocence, insouciance, and simple faith. . . . The New Testament world was not sentimental about children and had no illusion about any pretended innate goodness in them. . . . In the New Testament times, the child was considered of no importance, meriting little attention or favor. Children in that society had no status at all—they did not count.[10]

Under the Roman law of *patria potestas*, the father held complete control over every part of his child's life. If a first-century father did not want his newborn child, he "exposed" the infant—he left the baby to die in a deserted field. Children could neither possess their own property nor choose their own mates. Even when a child was grown, the patriarch of the household could legally exile or execute his offspring. Whether a child lived or died, ate or starved, succeeded or failed—*everything* in a child's life depended on the will of his or her father.[11]

The life of childlike trust in our heavenly Father has been described in this way: "It is recognizing one's nothingness, expecting everything from the good God, just as a little child expects everything from its father; it is not getting anxious about anything. . . . It is never being disheartened by one's faults, because children often fall, but they are too little to do themselves much harm."[12] To pray as a child is to pray as if everything in my life depends on my heavenly Father. Then, I no longer need to look for "your Kingdom come" for God's Kingdom has come in me.

LIVING IN DEPENDENCE ON MY FATHER

So, what does it mean to live in absolute dependence on my heavenly Father? I think we find the answer not in any teachings about prayer but in an unexpected time and an unlikely place—in the tormented cries of Yeshua in the Garden of Gethsemane (Mark 14:35–36). In the words of Walter Wangerin,

> What takes place in the Garden of Gethsemane is the Lord's Prayer actually *happening*, as though the earlier words were a script and this is the drama itself. . . . In the garden, Jesus, now more than ever in his ministry is the living embodiment of the second petition, *Thy kingdom come*. Right now, his acceptance of the Father's will *is* the coming of the kingdom here. And he begins both prayers the same. But whereas the first might have seemed a formal address to "Our Father," this latter cry is a howl, a spontaneous, needful plea: "*Abba*, Father!" Here is a child who cannot survive apart from this relationship. By crying "*Abba!*" he hurls himself at the holy parent: he runs like a child; like a child he begs attention but also like a child he trusts his daddy to do right and well.[13]

If the prayers in the garden *are* the disciples' prayers in action, it was the Prayer of the *Talmidim* that led Yeshua to the Hill of the Skull. At this point, this prayer is still a source of comfort, yet it also terrifies me. If Yeshua prayed, "*Abba,* thy will be done," and ended up on an execution stake, what might the prayer of the disciples cost me?

My dependence on myself? It cannot coexist with *Abba*, the word that declares my absolute dependence on the heavenly Father.

My obsession with titles to list behind my signature and accomplishments to adorn my *curriculum vitae*? They must crumble under the weight of the holiness of God's Name.

My longing for larger numbers to scribble on line seven of my 1040 form? It cannot stand when I sincerely pray for "daily bread"—what I need for the present moment, nothing more.

My conviction that I have the right to withhold forgiveness from the not-quite-divine people in my congregation? "Forgive us . . . as we too have forgiven those who have wronged us" shatters that delusion.

My flirtations with the fringes of sin? They cannot remain when I pray, "Keep us safe from the Evil One."

That's what it means to embrace the presence of the Kingdom in Yeshua *HaMashiach* (Jesus the Messiah), to embark on the journey to "your Kingdom come."

A Costly Journey

A few weeks ago, I received an advertisement from a prominent publisher. The heading declared, "Risk-free devotional materials!" If I am honest with myself, that's what I want sometimes when I repeat the Prayer of the *Talmidim*—a painless prayer that comforts me but never challenges me, a risk-free recitation to hang on my wall. Yet that is precisely what the Disciples' Prayer *isn't*. The prayer of the disciples is risky. Its demands are unnatural, unreasonable, and uncomfortable. It is not a prayer for the faint-hearted. Neither is it a prayer for individuals who want all the pleasures of a trip to hell without any of the unpleasant side effects. When we pray, "Our Father in heaven, . . . Your Kingdom come," we embark on a brutal journey that will not end until eternity begins. The journey is brutal because our Father refuses to postpone his kingdom until the end of time. To pray the Prayer of the *Talmidim* is to recognize that our Father wants to be fully present, here and now, in us.

> We do well not to pray the Lord's [Disciples'] Prayer lightly. It takes guts to pray it at all. . . . "Thy will be done" is what we are saying. . . . We are asking God to be God. We are asking God to do not what we want but what God wants. . . . "Thy kingdom come . . . on earth" is what we are saying. And if that were to suddenly happen, what then? What would stand and what would

fall? . . . Which if any of our most precious visions of who God is and of what human beings are would prove to be more or less on the mark and which would turn out to be phony as three-dollar bills? . . . It is only the words "Our Father" that make the prayer bearable. If God is indeed something like a father, then as something like children maybe we can risk approaching him anyway.[14]

A MEDITATION

Our Father in the heavens,
When I only call you "my God,"
I can live under the delusion that you are my property.
When I only call you "my King,"
I can live under the delusion that I am your prince.
Only when I whisper "our *Abba*," "our Father,"
do I know who I am.
I am *Abba*'s child.
Nothing more.
Nothing less.
Simply, only, *Abba*'s little boy.
Grimy face, grubby hands from building my own kingdoms—
they always crumble, mud and sand,
when your Kingdom washes over them.
I didn't like them either,
but your Kingdom seemed so far away.
Please, *Abba*, make your Kingdom come in me.

Chapter Six

When Words Are Not Enough—
Receiving the Gift of a God Who Sees Our Tears

PRAYERS AT THE TOMB OF LAZARUS

On arrival, Yeshua found that El'azar [Lazarus] had already been in the tomb for four days. . . . Yeshua, again deeply moved, came to the tomb. It was a cave, and a stone was lying in front of the entrance. . . . They removed the stone. Yeshua looked upward and said, "Father, I thank you that you have heard me. I myself know that you always hear me, but I say this because of the crowd standing around, so that they may believe that you have sent me." Having said this, he shouted, "El'azar! Come out!" The man who had been dead came out, his hands and feet wrapped in strips of linen and his face covered with a cloth. Yeshua said to them, "Unwrap him, and let him go!" (John 11:17, 38, 41–44)

Magnified and sanctified be His great name in the world which He created according to His will. And may He establish his kingdom during your life and during your days, and during the life of all the house of Israel, speedily and in the near future. . . . Blessed, praised and glorified, exalted, extolled and honored, adored and lauded be the Name of the Holy One, blessed be He, beyond all blessings and hymns, praises and songs that are uttered in the world.

From the *Kaddish*[1]

The band of learners meandered behind their teacher, up the southeastern slope of the Mount of Olives. After two days of traveling, they finally caught sight of Bethany. Still, no one spoke. The followers stared silently toward the village, squinting their eyes in the late afternoon sun. The rabbi told no riddles, Shim'on spoke no confessions, Ya'akov had no jokes, and Yochanan had no questions—none that he knew how to ask, anyway.

Suddenly, Shim'on heard the rhythmic slapping of sandal soles on the road that led to Bethany. When he looked up, he saw a woman in the distance, sprinting toward them like a frightened hare.

It was Miryam.

Miryam, the sister of Marta.

Miryam, the one whose brother was dead.

Shim'on watched the puffs of dust rise and fade beneath her feet as she ran down the dusty road. When Rabbi Yeshua saw her face, his chin quivered beneath his beard. Her eyes were bloodshot and swollen, and her sackcloth tunic was torn. Sweat and tears had mingled with the ashes on her cheeks until her skin became deathly gray. When she reached the teacher, she lunged forward and seized his feet.

"My Lord . . ." It was the ragged gasp of a woman who had wept until no tears remained. "If only you had been here, my brother . . . my brother wouldn't have died."

Yeshua slid to his knees, and Miryam fell, heaving, against his chest. The carpenter's hands gently soothed the tangled hair that had slipped from beneath her veil.

Miryam sobbed and moaned, but her eyes remained dry. "If only . . . if only . . . oh Lazarus!"

Within moments, the cries of the mourners and the wailing of flutes surrounded Yeshua's followers.[2] The mourners pitched dust in the air, the flutists performed their dirges, and the carpenter from Nazareth buried his face in his hands. The lamentations echoed around Miryam and her teacher: "May the Master of consolations comfort you!" "Blessed be the one who comforts the mourners!"[3]

"Where did you lay him?" Yeshua murmured.

"Lord." It was Marta who answered. "Come and see."

Yeshua stood and lifted Miryam to her feet. When he looked into her eyes, grief surged from the depths of his body. His shoulders began to convulse, and his chin dropped to his chest. He clutched the two sisters, as if he would collapse without them. The threesome stumbled toward the garden arm-in-arm, a living chain of sorrow.

When they reached the garden, the rabbi turned to a nearby mourner. "Run ahead and roll away the stone." The man was gone before Marta could protest.

"Lord, it's too late for you to see him now. He has been dead . . ." Marta choked on her words. When she recovered her voice, a hint of bitterness burst from the lump in her throat. "He has been dead for four days. The tomb already reeks!"

"I told you," his voice was firm and strong despite his tears, "if you believe, you will see God's glory."

The stone was already gone when they reached the garden. A dark, gaping hole stared at the crowd of mourners. When Miryam and Marta saw the open tomb, they crumpled to the ground. Only Yeshua remained standing.

He looked upward and declared, "Father, I thank you that you have heard me. I myself know that you always hear me, but I say this because of the crowd standing around, so that they may believe that you have sent me." When he turned from the tomb, even the birds were silent.

The look in the teacher's eyes shifted from sorrow to defiance.

Without warning, he lifted his hands and cried, "Lazarus! Come out!"

Marta bristled at the carpenter's callousness. Miryam simply cried . . . until she heard an unfamiliar rustling and dared to stare once more into the mouth of the cave. Someone was standing inside the tomb. What she saw didn't stop her tears—the tears, in fact, continued for several days—but the reason for her weeping changed.

THE LISTENING GOD

My wife's intentions were good. To celebrate the birthday of a certain *Star Wars* fanatic whom she had recently married, she baked a cookie in the shape of an Imperial Star Destroyer. I had asked for a *Star Wars* cake, so when I saw the resulting conglomeration of sugary dough, gray-blue icing, and chocolate chips, I laughed and thanked her several times. It was a thoughtful gift; I appreciated it—and it *did* look like a starship!

Unfortunately, the similarities between the cookie and a Star Destroyer didn't stop with the outward appearance. The taste and texture of the cookie were more like the titanium hull of a starship than I care to recall. And the smell . . . well, I've never actually sniffed the exhaust from a hyper-drive, but I'm sure this scent was fairly close. Somewhere between the mixing bowl and the table, something had gone desperately wrong with this culinary endeavor. After two days of chewing, the dog deduced that it was a Mesozoic fossil and returned it to the bowels of the earth where it belonged.

Despite the damage to my digestive system, I was thankful for Rayann's gift. Why? Because she had listened to my request. As I reflected on the incident, it occurred to me that perhaps my heavenly Father yearns for me to respond in the same way. He doesn't want me to thank him because he always gives me what I want—after all, he *doesn't* always give me what I want. He wants me to thank him because he has taken the time to listen to me. He wants to hear my prayers of gratitude not because of *what he gives* but because of *who he is.*

That's why the prayer that was spoken at the tomb of his Lazarus is so significant: "Father, I thank you that you have heard me. I myself know that you always hear me, but I say this because of the crowd standing around, so that they may believe that you have sent me." Yeshua didn't speak this prayer of gratitude after Lazarus lurched into the garden, full of life. When he prayed this prayer, the body of Lazarus was still decomposing in the darkness of a cave. After four days among the dead, Lazarus was a reeking mass of half-decayed flesh.

So if Lazarus was still dead, why did Yeshua thank his Father?

Was it because he was certain that his Father would raise Lazarus from the dead? I don't think so. Believe it or not, Yeshua didn't always receive positive responses to his prayers. Remember the prayer that the rabbi from Nazareth prayed for his future followers? "I pray not only for these, but also for those who will trust in me because of their word, that they may all be one. . . . The glory which you have given to me, I have given to them; so that they may be one, just as we are one—I united with them and you with me, so that they may be completely one" (John 17:20–23). Take one glance at the history of relations between followers of the Messiah, and you'll quickly discover how far God's people are from a positive answer to his prayer. Remember Yeshua's prayer in the garden? "'*Abba!*' (that is, 'Dear Father!') 'All things are possible for you. Take this cup away from me! Still, not what I want, but what you want'" (Mark 14:36). Yeshua's Father heard this prayer and answered this prayer—and the answer was *no*.

When Yeshua asked his Father to raise Lazarus from the dead, he had no guarantee that the answer would be *yes*. All he had was an assurance that his Father would do whatever it took to cause his identity to be, in the words of the ancient prayer that had been prayed at the tomb a few days earlier, "exalted and sanctified in the world that he created as he willed" (cf. John 11:4, 40; 12:27–28).

If impending resurrection wasn't the prime motive for Yeshua's prayer of gratitude, why did he thank his Father? The answer is simply this: He thanked God for hearing him—nothing more, nothing less. "Father," he prayed, "thank you for having heard me . . . you always hear me."

So what was it that God had heard? Was it Yeshua's promise to Marta that she would see God's glory? (see John 11:40). No, this promise to Marta wasn't a prayer. Was it a prayer for the resurrection of Lazarus that John somehow didn't happen to record in his retelling of Yeshua's life? Given that this text follows the Messiah's actions with such detail, that doesn't seem very plausible to me. Here's the answer that is, I believe, more probable than either of these options: Yeshua thanked his Father for hearing his tears.

Chaos had erupted around the tomb of Lazarus. The mourners wailed their words of comfort while the flutists played their mourning songs. The sisters felt abandoned and Yeshua's followers felt afraid. And the Messiah? According to Scripture, "Yeshua cried" (John 11:35). When Yeshua found himself in the shadow of his friend's tomb, he couldn't put his prayers into words, so he put them into tears instead. And his Father heard his cries. In some sense, this prayer became the means by which God answered the *Kaddish*, the prayer that had been prayed earlier at the tomb of Lazarus. The initial request of the *Kaddish* is that God's name be "magnified and sanctified . . . in the world which He created"—and through the tearful prayer of Yeshua, it did.

Ever been there? Ever found yourself trembling in the waiting room of a hospital, unable to pray but fully able to cry? Ever found that the familiar psalms and prayers that echo in your ears at the funeral simply can't capture the depth of your sorrow?

Even when our minds can't find the words to express our desires, our tears find a way to express our despair. The implication of Yeshua's prayer of gratitude is that God hears these unspoken prayers too. Romans 8:26 states: " . . . the Spirit helps us in our weakness; for we don't know how to pray the way we should. But the Spirit himself pleads on our behalf with groanings too deep for words."

I think that's why Yeshua prayed, "Father, I thank you that you have heard me." It wasn't because of any answer that his Father had given him—he hadn't received any answer yet. It wasn't because he knew that he would kiss his friend again before the day ended—he didn't have any guarantee that he would. No, he prayed this prayer because, amid the chaos and confusion of a crowd that couldn't see beyond the coldness of Lazarus' corpse, God heard the sobs of his Son. Not only did he hear this garbled prayer, but he also answered—and his reply flooded the tomb of Lazarus with more life than any cave on earth could possibly contain. From a cosmic perspective, a few tears shed over a single corpse seem fairly insignificant. Yet, in the plan of God, these tears became a prayer that was worthy of being answered.

GOD AND OUR "STUPID PROBLEMS"

Basketball bad boy Dennis Rodman once commented, "If there is a supreme being, he/she/it has a hell of a lot more to worry about than my stupid problems."[4] And he was right: God *does* have more important issues to deal with than my pathetic troubles.

Why should the one whose fingertips swirl solar systems around their suns listen to me blubber about my shattered dreams?

Why should the one who dances with the supernovas stop to hear me weep?

Why should the one who left the splendors of the angelic hosts to live upon this earth care about the paltry paroxysms of my soul?

Why should God pay attention to me?

The honest answer to these questions is that *he shouldn't*. Yet, the message of Yeshua's prayer is that *he does*. For reasons I still haven't figured out, my "stupid problems" are precisely what God *is* concerned about. In fact, the pangs and problems of this world concern God so deeply that when he stood face-to-face with them, he cried.

> This is a world where robins die, and sparrows, and people: the ones we love, the ones Jesus loves. All of them. They fall to the ground, they are enfolded into

the earth. And most times, Jesus doesn't come to raise them up, not in our lifetime, not so that we see. . . . And where is Jesus—this one "who was to come into the world?" What does Jesus think? What does Jesus feel about a world like this? "Jesus wept."[5]

Yes, Yeshua wept—but he did more than weep. He thanked his Father for hearing his sobs and for turning them into a prayer. And in the moments when tears flow more readily than words, we too can offer thanks, not because we've received what we wanted but because our Father sees our tears.

Living the Prayer

When I served our congregation as a minister to students, there was one sure-fire way to find me in the crowded hallways of our congregation's buildings—look for the seventh- and eighth-grade girls. For a couple of years, a gaggle of middle-school girls followed me wherever I went. I knew at least part of the reason that they followed me. Whenever they wanted to go to the mall, or play laser tag, or get some pizza, I and my wife would take them, because, when it comes to the pleadings of a little girl, I am—in the words of my wife—a total pushover. But then I noticed something peculiar. Even when I didn't have cash for pizza or the time to play games with them, they still tagged along.

One weekend, I asked a seventh-grader named Mandi, "Why do you still hang around, even I can't do anything fun?"

"It's 'cause, you . . ." Mandi wrinkled her nose and thought for a moment, ". . . you treat us like real people, even though we're really just a bunch of kids. You listen to us. So, we just tag along anyway."

Is that, perhaps, how I should look at God? He doesn't always take me where I want to go, and he doesn't always spend his riches according to my requests. Sometimes his answers to my prayers bring joy, and sometimes his answers are as tough and bitter as a charred chocolate-chip cookie. But he *does* always listen to me. And so I keep tagging along behind him—even when his answer to my request is *no*. Why? Perhaps it's because at the secret heart of all our prayers, what we really want is not an answer but an assurance—an assurance that our Father is listening. The prayer that was prayed at the tomb in Bethany is our assurance that he is.

A MEDITATION

My Father . . .
Can you hear me?
Are you listening?
Or do you have more pressing matters to attend to?
A choir rehearsal with the angel Gabriel, perhaps?
A strategy session meeting with archangel Michael?
A review of the newly born solar systems?
Aren't they more significant than my pathetic pleas?
Yet . . . you *are* listening, aren't you?
You really *hear* me, don't you?
You're paying attention to *me*!
I thought you would have better taste.
I thought you would have the sense to ignore
people like me.
But you don't,
And I am *so* glad.
Thank you, Father, for listening to
people who don't deserve to be heard.
Thank you, Father, for listening to
people like me.

PART III

Knowing the God Who Creates Community

Following the Messiah is tough—
God knows, it's too tough to do alone.
That's why Yeshua didn't call isolated individuals to
    follow him.
He called a group. He gathered a crowd.[1]

God is still gathering that crowd,
still pulling us together,
still trying to make us one,
by calling us to remember his sacrifice on our behalf,
by filling us with the Spirit of his holiness,
and by interceding on our behalf through his blessed Son.

Chapter Seven

The God Who Remembers—
Finding Community in our Memory of the Past

PESACH (PASSOVER) BLESSINGS AND PRAYERS

Why is this night different from all other nights? On all other nights we eat leavened or unleavened bread; on this night we eat only unleavened bread. On all other nights we eat all sorts of herbs; on this night we eat only bitter herbs. On all other nights we eat meat roasted, stewed, or boiled, on this night we eat only roasted meat. Why is this night different from all other nights?

My father was a nomad from Aram. He went down into Egypt with meager numbers and sojourned there. There he became a great and very populous nation. The Egyptians dealt harshly with us and oppressed us. They imposed heavy labor on us. We cried to *Adonai* the God of our ancestors, and *Adonai* heard our plea and saw our plight, our pain, and our oppression. *Adonai* freed us from Egypt by a mighty hand, by an outstretched arm, and awesome power, and with signs and wonders.

This is the sacrifice of the *Pesach* of *Adonai*, for he passed over the houses of the people of Israel in Egypt when he slaughtered the Egyptians but spared our houses. We were Pharaoh's slaves in Egypt, and *Adonai* our God brought us forth from there with a mighty hand and an outstretched arm. And if the Holy One, may he be blessed, had not brought our ancestors out of Egypt, then we, our children and our grandchildren, would still be Pharaoh's slaves in Egypt.

Question and Response from the Passover *Seder*[2]

Blessed be *Adonai* our God, king of the universe, who in his goodness feeds the whole world with grace, kindness, and mercy. He gives food to all flesh, for his kindness is everlasting. Blessed be *Adonai* our God who provides food for all.

We thank you, *Adonai* our God, for having given our ancestors a heritage—a precious, good, and spacious land; for having brought us out from the land of Egypt and redeemed us from the house of slavery; for your covenant which you have sealed in our flesh; for your *Torah* which you have taught us; for your statutes which you have revealed to us; for the life, favor, and kindness which you have graciously given to us; and for the food we eat with which you constantly feed and sustain us every day, at all times, and at every hour.

Our God and the God of our ancestors, may there rise and come and approach and be seen, accepted, heard, recollected, and remembered, the remembrance of us and the recollection of us, and the remembrance of our ancestors, and the remembrance of the Messiah, the descendant of David your servant, and the remembrance of Jerusalem, your holy city, and the remembrance of all your people, the house of Israel. May their remembrance come before you for life and for peace on this Festival of Unleavened Bread.

Birkat HaMazon[3]
Blessing Spoken at the Passover Meal

Were they ready?

I was only the serving boy that night, but I had done all that I could to make the room ready for the *seder*. I glanced around the wooden doorframe. Oil lamps tossed shadows carelessly across the walls of the Upper Room. The rabbi and his followers had finished their first cup of wine. Now, they reclined around the table on linen cushions stuffed with wool.

"I tell you," Yeshua was saying, "whoever receives anyone whom I send receives me. And whoever receives me receives the one who sent me."

Was it time to serve the first course?

The rabbi nodded.

I lifted the platter and made my way to the head of the table. Vinegar and wine, roasted lamb and a stack of bread, *maror* (bitter herbs) and the sour-sweet *charoset* (apple-nut mixture). The scents swirled around me, and for a moment, the slaves who celebrated the first *Pesach* in Egypt didn't seem that far away. One by one, the men at the table dabbled the bitter herbs into a cup of vinegar and swallowed the bitterness or our bondage.

Yeshua lifted the wineskin from the platter, and I retreated to a darkened corner. As he poured the crimson liquid into a large cup, the *talmid* (disciple) named Yochanan asked the familiar questions:

> "Why is this night different from all other nights? On all other nights we eat leavened or unleavened bread; on this night we eat only unleavened bread. On all other nights we eat all sorts of herbs; on this night we eat only bitter herbs. On all other nights we eat meat roasted, stewed, or boiled; on this night we eat only roasted meat. Why is this night different from all other nights?"[4]

Yeshua was silent for a moment as he stared into his cup of wine and water, as if he noticed something in the crimson liquid to which the rest of us were blind. Finally, he began to repeat the familiar story:

> "My father was a nomad from Aram. He went down into Egypt with meager numbers and sojourned there.

There he became a great and very populous nation. The
Egyptians dealt harshly with us and oppressed us. They
imposed heavy labor on us. We cried to *Adonai* the God
of our ancestors, and *Adonai* heard our plea and saw
our plight, our pain, and our oppression. *Adonai* freed
us from Egypt by a mighty hand, by an outstretched
arm and awesome power, and with signs and wonders.
If the Holy One had not brought our ancestors out of
Egypt, then we, our children, and our grandchildren
would still be Pharaoh's slaves in Egypt."⁵

The teacher sat up, raised his hands, and began to chant the
hallel (praise psalms). One by one, his followers joined in the song:

Halleluyah! Servants of ADONAI, give praise! Give praise
to the name of ADONAI! Blessed be the name of ADONAI
from this moment on and forever! From sunrise until
sunset ADONAI's name is to be praised. ADONAI is high
above all nations, his glory above the heavens. Who is
like ADONAI our God, seated in the heights, humbling
himself to look on heaven and on earth. He raises the
poor from the dust, lifts the needy from the rubbish
heap, in order to give him a place among princes,
among the princes of his people. He causes the childless
woman to live at home happily as a mother of children.
Halleluyah!⁶

Yeshua handed the cup to Judas. One by one, the men around
the table drank the wine—everyone except Yeshua.⁷ As Yeshua and
his followers washed their hands, I returned the platter to the head
of the table. It was time for the meal.

Yeshua reached for one of the flat cakes and intoned the
blessing: "Blessed be *Adonai* our God who brings forth bread from
the earth. Blessed be *Adonai* our God who has sanctified us with his
commands and commanded us concerning the eating of *matzah*."

When the rabbi broke the piece of *matzah*, his chin fell to his
chest and a moan escaped his lips, as if someone had suddenly
struck him. I barely heard him murmur, "Truly, I tell you . . . one of
you . . . will . . . hand me over . . . to them."

"No!" Shim'on jumped to his feet. "Never!"
The others at the table echoed Shim'on's cry.
"Surely not I!"
Yochanan whispered something in the rabbi's ear. I couldn't hear Yeshua's reply, but when he stood up, the room turned deathly quiet. Yeshua dipped a broken bit of bread with a piece of bitter herb into the bowl of crushed figs, nuts, and vinegar. He handed the bread, still dripping with *charoset*, to Judas and said softly, "Do quickly what you are going to do."

Silence.

Judas grabbed his sandals and lunged toward the door. He clutched the doorpost for a few moments before running down the steps and into the night. The piece of bread was still clenched in his fist. He never stopped to put on his sandals.

What had just happened? I wasn't alone in my wondering. No one present seemed certain about what had just taken place. Perhaps that's why everyone ate in such silence. The meal, the washing of the hands, the pouring of the third cup of wine . . . if anyone spoke, it was in a whisper. When the last bit of flesh had been torn from the bones of the lamb, Yeshua broke the silence. He began to recite the *Birkat HaMazon*:

This is the bread of affliction that our ancestors ate when they came out of Egypt.

Blessed be *Adonai* our God, king of the universe, who in his goodness feeds the whole world with grace, kindness, and mercy. He gives food to all flesh, for his kindness is everlasting. Blessed be *Adonai* our God who provides food for all.

We thank you, *Adonai* our God, for having given our ancestors a heritage—a precious, good, and spacious land; for having brought us out from the land of Egypt and redeemed us from the house of slavery; for your covenant which you have sealed in our flesh; for your *Torah* which you have taught us; for your statutes which you have revealed to us; for the life, favor, and kindness which you have graciously given

to us; and for the food we eat with which you constantly feed and sustain us every day, at all times, and
at every hour.

Our God and the God of our ancestors, may there rise
and come and approach and be seen, accepted, heard,
recollected, and remembered, the remembrance of us
and the recollection of us, and the remembrance of
our ancestors, and the remembrance of the Messiah,
the descendant of David your servant, and the
remembrance of Jerusalem, your holy city, and the
remembrance of all your people, the house of Israel.
May their remembrance come before you for life and
for peace on this Festival of Unleavened Bread.

The rabbi grasped the last piece of bread and ripped the bread into
two jagged chunks. Were those drops of sweat that I saw, glistening
like tiny stars beneath his eyes? Or were they tears?

"Take it, eat it," he commanded. "This is my body, which is
being given for you; do this in memory of me." Yochanan tore off a
small piece and looked upward, his eyes full of questions that he
did not know how to ask. The rabbi nodded. Yochanan placed the
piece of bread on his tongue and passed the chunk to Ya'akov. Each
of the *talmidim* broke a piece of bread from the chunk and chewed
it, but no one seemed to know why.

Yeshua raised the third cup of wine and spoke the familiar
blessing: "Blessed be *Adonai*, who created the fruit of the vine."

The cup of wine shook slightly in his hands.

He spoke in short, ragged bursts: "All of you, drink from it! For
this is my blood, which ratifies the New Covenant, my blood shed
on behalf of many, so that they may have their sins forgiven. I tell
you, I will not drink this 'fruit of the vine' again until the day I
drink new wine with you in my Father's Kingdom." The *talmidim*
sipped the warm wine, slowly, tentatively, uncertainly.

On every other *Pesach* celebration that I had ever experienced,
we sang and laughed at the end of the meal. But on this night,
though we still sang the last psalms of the *hallel*, there was no
laughter. There was only a strange silence, as if we were waiting for
some unexpected guest that we had never met before.

A NIGHT OF MEMORIES

What made the *Pesach seder* so special?

It certainly wasn't the quality of the food. An ancient *Pesach* platter would not have been the most appetizing meal. The vegetables were bitter and the bread was bland.

What made the *seder* special wasn't the meal—it was the memory. It was as if, once each year, God sat down at the table with his people, opened a tattered scrapbook, and recounted the story of his relationship with them: "See that whiskered Aramean, staring over the horizon? He was a wandering man. No one ever could get him to settle in one place for very long, but I turned him into a mighty nation. He was your ancestor. Don't forget about him.

"Here's a postcard with an Egyptian postmark. It's from the time when your people were slaves. They begged me to save them. So when the time was right, I rolled up my sleeves and rescued them. If I hadn't brought your ancestors out of Egypt, you'd be on the night shift right now, making bricks from mud and straw. Don't forget about them.

"Oh, and look at this picture! See the blood around the doors? That's from the night that every firstborn Egyptian died, but the angel of death passed over all the Hebrew households. That was the night when there wasn't time to leaven the bread or boil the lamb—you knew that God was going to rescue you, so you had to be ready to leave. Don't forget that evening."

The *Birkat HaMazon* picked up on the theme of remembering. The closing lines of the prayer are:

> Our God and the God of our ancestors, may there . . .
> be seen, accepted, heard, recollected, and remembered,
> the remembrance of us and the recollection of us, and
> the remembrance of our ancestors, and the
> remembrance of the Messiah . . . and the remembrance
> of Jerusalem, your holy city, and the remembrance of
> all your people, the house of Israel. May their
> remembrance come before you for life and for peace on
> this Feast of Unleavened Bread.

In this prayer God's people were saying, "Oh, God, don't forget the story we share. Remember the covenant you made with our ancestors. Remember to send the Messiah. Remember the holy city. And, most of all, please remember *us*."

And God did.

I don't think it's a coincidence that the next command spoken by Yeshua after he prayed the *Birkat HaMazon* at the Last *Seder* was, "Do this in remembrance of me."[8] It was as if Yeshua were telling his followers, "Not only did I remember my covenant with your ancestors; I am renewing my covenant and signing it in my own blood. Not only did I remember to send the Messiah—I myself *became* the Messiah. Not only did I remember the holy city—I am turning *you* into a holy city.[9] I have remembered you. Now, you remember me."

So we do.

IT'S NOT ABOUT THE MEAL; IT'S ABOUT THE MEMORY

Millions of believers throughout the world continue to remember the events that transpired during Yeshua's final Passover *seder*, before his execution. Some call it Communion; others call it the Lord's Supper. Some share a common loaf; others eat wafers; still others eat *matzah*. Some sip from a common cup; others drink from tiny glasses that look like transparent thimbles; still others drink from full cups, such as the ones used at a Passover *seder*.

Why do so many people continue to partake of this ritual? In order to commemorate and remember the God who has chosen never to forget us. "I have engraved you on the palms of my hands," God once promised his people, "your walls are always before me" (Isa. 49:16).

In Yeshua *HaMashiach*, God fulfilled that promise. God promised never to forget his people, and his promise has been engraved in heaven—not in the splendor of silver and gold, but in the frailty of human flesh.

God has carved the memory of us into the body of his Son—in the crimson craters that mar his feet and hands, in the gaping hole in his side, in the ragged gashes that crisscross his back, in the scars that still crown his skull.

Now, when we pray, "may there . . . be seen, accepted, heard, recollected, and remembered, the remembrance of us," we have the assurance that we *have* been remembered, once and for all. That's what the celebration of this ritual commemorates. It's not about the dry bread that sticks in our throats or the purple-tinged drink that stains our clothes. It's about the God who has chosen to remember us through the body and blood of his one and only Son.

Ever feel like God has forgotten you?

Look at the bread and the wine.

See his blood in the cup?

See his scars in the *matzah*?

He *can't* forget you.

A MEDITATION

My Redeemer,
"Remember me
when you enter your kingdom."
That's what the felon beside you asked.
A few hours earlier,
that's what you had asked your Father . . .
"Remember us."
Did the felon know that when he turned his head
and saw your broken body,
he was seeing God's answer
to the prayers of the Passover?
Is that why you replied,
"Today, you will be with me in Paradise?"
You didn't look like much of an answer to prayer.
But you were.
Thank you, my bruised and broken Messiah,
for engraving the memory of me
in the palms of your hands,
in the bones of your feet,
in the hollow in your side,
in the crown of your skull,
in your sacred, pierced heart.
Thank you, my Redeemer,
for remembering me.

Chapter Eight

The God Who is One—
Finding Community in the Unity of God

THE PRAYER FOR UNITY

After Yeshua had said these things, he looked up toward heaven and said, "Father, the time has come. Glorify your Son, so that the Son may glorify you—just as you gave him authority over all mankind, so that he might give eternal life to all those whom you have given him. And eternal life is this: to know you, the one true God, and him whom you sent, Yeshua the Messiah.

"I glorified you on earth by finishing the work you gave me to do. Now, Father, glorify me alongside yourself. Give me the same glory I had with you before the world existed.

"I made your name known to the people you gave me out of the world. They were yours, you gave them to me, and they have kept your word. Now they know that everything you have given me is from you, because the words you gave me I have given to them, and they have received them. They have really come to know that I came from you, and they have come to trust that you sent me.

"I am praying for them. I am not praying for the world, but for those you have given to me, because they are yours. Indeed, all I have is yours, and all you have is mine, and in them I have been glorified. Now I am no longer in the world. They are in the world, but I am coming to you. Holy Father, guard them by the power of your name, which you have given to me, so that they may be one, just as we are. When I was with them, I guarded them by the power of your name, which you have given to me; yes, I kept watch over them; and not one of them was destroyed (except the one meant for destruction, so that the *Tanakh* might be fulfilled). . . .

"I pray not only for these, but also for those who will trust in me because of their word, that they may all be one. Just as you, Father, are united with me and I with you, I pray that they may be united with us, so that the world may believe that you sent me. The glory which you have given to me, I have given to them; so that they may be one, just as we are one—I united with them and you with me, so that they may be completely one, and the world thus realize that you sent me, and that you have loved them just as you have loved me.

"Father, I want those you have given me to be with me where I am; so that they may see my glory, which you have given me because you loved me before the creation of the world. Righteous Father, the world has not known you, but I have known you, and these people have known that you sent me. I made your name known to them, and I will continue to make it known; so that the love with which you have loved me may be in them, and I myself may be united with them."

After Yeshua had said all this, he went out with his *talmidim* across the stream that flows in winter through the *Vadi Kidron* [Kidron Valley], to a spot where there was a grove of trees; and he and his *talmidim* went into it.

Then Yeshua went with his *talmidim* to a place called Gat-Sh'manim [Gethsemane] and said to them, "Sit here while I go over there and pray." (John 17:1–12; 17:20–18:1; Matthew 26:36)

The streets along the southern wall of Jerusalem were deserted and dark.

The faces in the torchlight were clenched like fists. Eyes wondering and wide. Skin clammy and cold. Feet stumbling occasionally in the fading sunlight.

"First, I left the Father and arrived in the world." Yeshua spoke softly to avoid attracting the attention of the Roman auxiliaries who were roaming the streets that night. "Now I am leaving the world to return to my Father."

"Finally!" James said. "You're talking plainly—you're not speaking indirectly anymore."

"Now we know that you know everything. No more questions from us!" Shim'on's tone was confident. "Now we believe that you came from God."

Yeshua whirled abruptly, eyes flashing, "Do you really believe now? The time is coming—no, it's already here!—when you will scatter, each one looking out for himself, and you'll leave me alone. But I am not really alone," he whispered. "The Father is with me."

The rabbi turned and continued walking. When his followers caught up with him, he told them, "I have said these things to you so that, inasmuch as you join your lives with mine, you will experience *shalom* [peace]. In this world, you'll experience trials. But be brave! I have already conquered the world."

When they reached the Ashpot Gate, Yeshua stopped and looked upward. His eyes closed and his face crinkled slightly as he began to pray.

Father, the time has come. Glorify your Son, so that the Son may glorify you—just as you gave him authority over all mankind, so that he might give eternal life to all those whom you have given him. And eternal life is this: to know you, the one true God, and him whom you sent, Yeshua the Messiah. I glorified you on earth by finishing the work you gave me to do. Now, Father, glorify me alongside yourself. Give me the same glory I had with you before the world existed.

I made your name known to the people you gave me out of the world. They were yours, you gave them to

me, and they have kept your word. Now they know that
everything you have given me is from you, because the
words you gave me I have given to them, and they have
received them. They have really come to know that I
came from you, and they have come to trust that you
sent me. I am praying for them. I am not praying for
the world, but for those you have given to me, because
they are yours. Indeed, all I have is yours, and all you
have is mine, and in them I have been glorified.

Now I am no longer in the world. They are in the
world, but I am coming to you. Holy Father, guard
them by the power of your name, which you have given
to me, so that they may be one, just as we are. When I
was with them, I guarded them by the power of your
name, which you have given to me; yes, I kept watch
over them; and not one of them was destroyed (except
the one meant for destruction, so that the *Tanakh* might
be fulfilled). But now, I am coming to you; and I say
these things while I am still in the world so that they
may have my joy made complete in themselves. I have
given them your word, and the world hated them,
because they do not belong to the world—just as I
myself do not belong to the world. I don't ask you to
take them out of the world, but to protect them from
the Evil One. They do not belong to the world, just as I
do not belong to the world.

Yeshua slipped through the Ashpot Gate and turned toward
the Mount of Olives. His followers traipsed behind him, straining
to hear, longing for a clue to help them understand what was
happening.

Set them apart for holiness by means of the truth—
your word is truth. Just as you sent me into the world, I
have sent them into the world. On their behalf I am
setting myself apart for holiness, so that they too may
be set apart for holiness by means of the truth.

I pray not only for these, but also for those who will trust in me because of their word, that they may all be one. Just as you, Father, are united with me and I with you, I pray that they may be united with us, so that the world may believe that you sent me. The glory which you have given to me, I have given to them; so that they may be one, just as we are one—I united with them and you with me, so that they may be completely one, and the world thus realize that you sent me, and that you have loved them just as you have loved me.

Father, I want those you have given me to be with me where I am; so that they may see my glory, which you have given me because you loved me before the creation of the world. Righteous Father, the world has not known you, but I have known you, and these people have known that you sent me. I made your name known to them, and I will continue to make it known; so that the love with which you have loved me may be in them, and I myself may be united with them.

The band of twelve trickled down the western slope of the Kidron Valley. The walls of Jerusalem loomed behind them, tossing dark shadows across the Mount of Olives.

Yeshua glanced to his left. Did anyone else notice the row of torches winding toward them, slipping from the Temple courts like a long, luminous serpent?

The teacher knew who stood at the head of the serpent. Only a few hours earlier, he'd washed the man's feet. Were they still clean?

The serpent continued to slither toward the Mount of Olives.

There was so little time.

A View Like None Other

Buried in the highlands of Scotland is a forested valley called Balquidder. In the ninth century c.e., a man named Angus glimpsed this lush, meandering depression in the earth. Overwhelmed by its breathtaking beauty, he declared it "a thin place"—a place where the separation between this world and the next was almost transparent.[1]

Thin places . . .

You've encountered them too.

In the gurgling cry of a newborn baby.

In the echo of the words of Yeshua, "Do this in memory of me."

In a sunset too beautiful to be explained by any science textbook.

All of them, thin places . . . places where heaven and earth don't seem that far apart.

Yeshua's prayer for unity as he made his way across the Kidron Valley is also a thin place. Through this prayer, we gain a tiny, glistening hint of the inner glory of God. And what we see at the center of God's being is not blinding light or raw power but a resplendent relationship. We see not simply how God relates *to us* but how the Father, Son, and Spirit relate *to one another.* Remember Yeshua's words?

> Now, Father, glorify me alongside yourself. Give me the same glory I had with you before the world existed. . . . Father, I want those you have given me to be with me where I am; so that they may see my glory, which you have given me because you loved me before the creation of the world. (John 17:5, 24)

Long before God burst into time through the birth canal of a peasant girl, the Father and the Son played soccer with the planets, danced with the Spirit of God, and simply, eternally, enjoyed the experience of being *God.* Through the "thin place" that this prayer provides, we glimpse the infinite, inner fellowship of God.

And we glimpse something else through this thin place—a profound longing within the deepest part of God to see his glorious love-relationship reflected among his people. Repeatedly, Yeshua prayed for the unity of his followers:

> Holy Father, guard them . . . so that they may be one just as we are. . . . I pray not only for these, but also for those who will trust in me because of their word, that they may all be one. . . . I pray that they may be united

with us. . . . The glory which you have given to me, I
have given to them; so that they may be one, just as we
are one. (John 17:11, 20–22)

"That they may all be one." "One just as we are." "United with
us." Not only does God long for unity among his people, but he
also has rooted that longing for unity in his own identity. The
phrase "one just as we are one" clearly echoes the *Sh'ma,* the ancient
Jewish confession of faith: "ADONAI our God, ADONAI is one!" (Deut.
6:4). God's motive for wanting his people to be one is the fact that
he himself is one.

Nevertheless, two thousand years after Yeshua prayed this
prayer, I see scant evidence that any of these pleas are being
answered. Denominations divide over dogmatic details, congregations draw lines based on social demographics, and individual believers ignore the longing for unity that flows from the
inner life of God. What we have forgotten is the same simple fact
that the earliest followers of Yeshua forgot more than once—*we
need one another.*

I NEED YOU, YOU NEED ME

Notice the plural pronouns of Yeshua's prayer:
"The words you gave me I have given to *them.*"
"The glory which you have given to me, I have given to *them.*"
"I united with *them* and you with me, so that *they* may be
completely one, and the world thus realize that . . . you have loved
them."

Not once in this prayer did Yeshua declare, "I gave *her* your
word," or "the glory which you have given to me, I have given to
him." Just as in the Disciples' Prayer, the context for faith is not the
experience of a lone individual. Faith in Yeshua the Messiah
requires a community of believers. It is neither "I" nor "me," neither
"him" nor "her"; it is always "we" and "us," "they" and "them."

If I take this prayer for unity seriously, I must give up the
arrogant illusion that my spiritual life and my sins are personal
matters. I must admit that I cannot follow Yeshua *HaMashiach*
alone any more than I can get married alone. To follow Yeshua, I
need the fellowship of other believers in Messiah. So do you, and so

has every believer throughout time. Faith in Yeshua is inherently communal. He "did not call isolated individuals to follow him. He called a group of disciples. He gathered a crowd." [2]

That's why it's not completely accurate to say that any of us has a "personal relationship with God." What we have is a *communal* relationship with God. I owe my understanding of Yeshua to the scribes who preserved the stories, to the martyrs who died for the stories, and to the teachers who repeated their stories.

Were these scribes and martyrs and teachers perfect? No, they were as imperfect as the men and women who make their way to thousands of other communities of faith each week. The scribes made some mistakes, the martyrs sinned, and by the end of classes, my teachers were inexplicable cranky. But I need every one of them.

Without the ancient scribes, I could never have experienced the raw honesty of the prophet Jeremiah or the concern for the downtrodden that has led me to cherish Luke's version of the life of Yeshua. Without the examples of the martyrs, it would be far more difficult for me to believe that Yeshua was truly raised from the dead. And, without the patience of teachers past and present, my faith in Yeshua would never have grown beyond the simple plea of a five-year-old boy: "I need to know Jesus."

THE MIRACULOUSLY MISMATCHED COMMUNITY

That's why I have no desire to join a congregation filled with people "just like me." If everyone's educational level, economic status, and racial profile were identical to mine, why would we need each other? Part of the "nonsense" of Yeshua's execution-stake is the fact that those who rub shoulders in the shadow of the hill where he died are the people that the world would never dream of blending together (see 1 Cor 1:18, 26).

When I gather to worship and to pray with others, I want to encounter a multitude that reminds me how Yeshua "ransomed for God persons from every tribe, language, people and nation" (Rev. 5:9). I want to shake brown hands and white hands, smooth hands and callused hands, wrinkled hands and tiny, trembling, newborn hands.

Why? Because life in the congregation of Yeshua is not about my personal tastes or desires. In fact, it's not about *me* at all. It is about belonging to a mismatched community of recovering sinners who have been bound together by a Spirit that no one has seen. C.S. Lewis wrote that in the first few weeks after becoming a believer:

> I thought that I could do it on my own, by retiring to my room and reading theology . . . I disliked very much [the songs that other believers sang in worship], which I considered to be fifth-rate poems set to sixth-rate music. But as I went on, I saw the great merit of it. I came up against different people of quite different outlooks and different education, and then gradually my conceit just began peeling off. I realized that the hymns . . . were, nevertheless, being sung with devotion and benefit by an old saint in elastic-side boots in the opposite pew, and then you realize that you aren't fit to clean those boots. It gets you out of your solitary conceit.[3]

To be "completely one" with other believers in Messiah means giving up our "solitary conceit," our foolish delusion that following Yeshua is something that we can do on our own.

THE REASON TO BELIEVE

The community of faith has a greater function than my personal spiritual development, though. Believe it or not, Yeshua left only one proof that he had spoken the truth. It wasn't logically sound— in fact, from my perspective, it doesn't seem very logical at all. It was the unity of his people. According to his prayer, "I pray . . . that they may all be one . . . so that the world may believe that you sent me" (John 17:20–21). Allow me to paraphrase his point: *The world will be won not through the wisdom of our words but through the witness of our oneness.*

I know, I know. It sounds pretty crazy to me too. Someone once commented that communities of faith are a lot like Noah's ark—if it weren't for the storm on the outside, no one could stand the fact that they smell like you-know-what on the inside. But what would happen if we focused less on the difficulties of being unified and more on the wondrous unity that God has modeled. According to Yeshua, our best hope for convincing the world that he was no ordinary human being is to reflect the inner nature of God—a nature in which the diversity of Father, Son, and Spirit coexist in perfect unity.

Suppose that we did constantly consider the fact that the way we commune with other followers of the Messiah is the primary proof of God's presence in Yeshua. Perhaps then the world would see that, despite its many failures, the community of believers in Yeshua *is* a wondrous miracle. It is loving and forgiving, laughing and weeping, worshiping and seeking God in the midst of this motley multitude of imperfect people.

What Was in That Cup?

Immediately after Yeshua prayed for the unity of his people, he entered into the Garden of Gethsemane. Remember the scene?

> They went to a place called Gat Sh'manim; and Yeshua said to his *talmidim*, "Sit here while I pray." He took with him Kefa [Peter], Ya'akov [James] and Yochanan [John]. Great distress and anguish came over him; and he said to them, "My heart is so filled with sadness that I could die! Remain here and stay awake." Going on a little farther, he fell on the ground and prayed that if possible, the hour might pass from him: "*Abba!*" (that is, "Dear Father!") "All things are possible for you. Take this cup away from me! Still, not what I want, but what you want." (Mark 14:32–36)

I wonder, was Yeshua's sorrow caused only by the agony that he was about to face? Or did he, perhaps, look forward in time and glimpse the disunity of his people? Did he see how poorly we have reflected the God who is One? Did he witness the controversies and the crusades that would shatter his body into thousands of competing sects? Did he hear the bitter backbiting that besmirches the fellowship in your congregation and in mine? Was that a part of his pain?

I don't know.

I do know this: Even if he didn't witness our disunity in the garden, he bore it on the hill of Calvary. For our disunity is sin.

Do we want the world to follow Yeshua? Philosophical apologetics are easier. Witnessing manuals are cheaper. But neither one provides the proof for which Yeshua himself prayed—"that they may all be one . . . so that the world may believe that you sent me" (John 17:21).

THE THIN PLACE

Would you like to experience the ultimate "thin place," where heaven and earth intersect? Would you like to see perfect unity among all who believe that Yeshua is the Messiah? (The world would *never* be able to explain away that one.) It starts with you. If you aren't certain where to begin, how about asking a believer that you can't stand to share a meal with you? No one ever said it would be easy.

A MEDITATION

Lord of all creation and Lord of your people,
It's easy to love my congregation.
It's not so easy to love certain members of my congregation.
You prayed to your Father,
"I want them to be one even as we are one."
You commanded your first followers,
"Love one another, just as I have loved you."
Did you really mean it?
Are you sure?
No exceptions?
Everyone?
Even . . . you-know-who?

Could it be that your words were a promise *and* a command?
When you commanded, "Love one another,"
were you also promising,
"You *will be able* to love one another?"
When you prayed, "I want them to be one,"
Were you also promising,
"They *will be able* to be one?"
I hope so.
Help me to see that I cannot honestly love you
unless I also love your people.
Even . . . you-know-who.
God, be merciful to me, a sinner—
this could take a while.

PART IV

Knowing the God Who Creates a New Future

Three truths—each embedded in a prayer.
God suffers with us—
"My God! My God! Why have you deserted me?"
God's favor rests upon us—
"May the Lord make his face to shine upon you."
God's glory is present in us—
"The glory that you have given me I have given them."

Three truths that form a new future
for those who call God "*Abba*"—
a future with a God
who comprehends his children's sorrows,
who shines on his children's lives,
who transforms his children to reflect
the infinite glory of his Son.

Chapter Nine

Praying in the Darkness—
Creating a New Future in the Face of Death

PRAYERS FROM THE EXECUTION-STAKE

Yeshua said, "Father, forgive them; they don't understand what they are doing." They divided up his clothes by throwing dice. From noon until three o'clock in the afternoon, all the Land was covered with darkness. At about three, Yeshua uttered a loud cry, "*Eli! Eli! L'mah sh'vaktani?* (My God! My God! Why have you deserted me?)" On hearing this, some of the bystanders said, "He's calling for Eliyahu [Elijah]." After this, knowing that all things had accomplished their purpose, Yeshua, in order to fulfill the words of the *Tanakh*, said, "I'm thirsty." A jar full of cheap sour wine was there; so they soaked a sponge in the wine, coated it with oregano leaves and held it up to his mouth. Crying out with a loud voice, Yeshua said, "Father! Into your hands I commit my spirit." After Yeshua had taken the wine, he said, "It is accomplished!" And, letting his head droop, he delivered up his spirit. (Selections from Matt. 27:45–47; Luke 23:34–35, 46; John 19:28–30)

Darkness.

Like a vast, black cloak unfolding in the eastern sky.

Darkness at noonday.[1]

Hollow, aching shadows, washing over the land until the hills become indistinct.

Formless.

Formless and void. As if God has hurled the cosmos back to the beginning and started over.

A whisper, from the crest of the hill: "Father, forgive them; they don't understand what they are doing."

A woman stands silently on the slope.[2] Despite the cluster of bodies around her, she stands alone in her sorrow. It isn't the first time. Only years of heartache can plow furrows in a woman's face like the ones that crisscross her forehead.

Miryam can no longer see the sun or moon. Every luminous sphere seems to have slipped from the sky. The only light is the horrible, haunting glow that smolders along the distant horizon. Still, it is enough, just enough to see her son.

Naked. Dangling from the iron spikes. Mangled, his gaping gashes covered with flies and congealed blood. His skull crudely crowned with a thorn bush. His robe—the robe that her hands had woven for him—now draped across the shoulders of a Roman auxiliary who stands at the crest of the hill.

The words of the white-robed messenger still echo in the recesses of Miryam's heart: "He will be great! He will rule the house of Jacob forever! His kingdom will never end." Perhaps he had been great, but he had never ruled a kingdom. He'd never even wanted one, it seemed. Yet she had never stopped hoping.

Until this morning. Until Zebedee's son screamed her name from the courtyard of the house in Bethany. Until she and Yochanan staggered up the Hill of the Skull and she glimpsed her son, spread-eagled beneath the sneering words on the placard nailed above him: "King of the Jews." If he is a king, his is a pathetic kingdom. His only throne is a bloody stake, stabbed into the Hill of the Skull, and his only soldier is an unarmed fisherman surrounded by a mob of sobbing women.

Miryam opens her eyes and sees nothing. Utter blackness has descended like a starving vulture, devouring every glimmer of light. How long has she stood in this darkness? Minutes or hours? Does it even matter? Time has ceased. Only infinite blackness remains.

"*Eli!*" a ragged shriek rips the silent void. "*Eli! L'mah sh'vaktani?*" A cry like no one has heard before. A cry from the depths of hell.

A voice that the woman on the hill knows too well. The voice of her son.

"My God! My God! Why have you deserted me?"

The woman crumples to the ground, retching, longing to expel the anguish that has torn her stomach in two. Too much . . . too much . . . it is too much. To the religious leaders, her son has been a nuisance, healing lepers one moment and hobnobbing with whores the next. To the Romans, he has been a threat—from their perspective; Galileans had an annoying habit of turning into violent revolutionaries. But to the woman on the hill, this man was always the flailing infant who suckled his life from her breast . . . the curly-haired toddler with the splinter in his palm . . . the boy whom she loved so deeply but who never truly belonged to her . . . the young man who wandered out of the carpentry shop one morning and never came back. Now he dangled from a splintered beam, his skin shredded by the whip, his wrists shattered by iron spikes, his dark eyes swollen and bruised.

The elderly priest in the Temple had warned her: "A sword will pierce your own heart." But she had never imagined that this would be part of the deal. "Dear God of my fathers," she moans, "what went wrong? How could I have saved him?"

When she raises her head, hints of sunlight frolic unevenly along the horizon, mocking her pain. One by one, jagged streaks of crimson and orange emerge until the western sky seems to be on fire, like the end of time—or was it the beginning?

Miryam barely hears her son's request: "I . . . thirst." A bystander plunges a grimy sponge into the Roman soldier's jug of *posca* (sour wine). He crumbles a few leaves on the sponge, mounts it on a branch, and rams it into Yeshua's face. The Galilean strains forward and gnaws the sponge desperately, drawing the acrid liquid into his swollen throat.[3]

Suddenly, Yeshua looks up, beyond Miryam, beyond the Holy City, as if he is searching for a certain, familiar face that has eluded him for too long.

"Father . . ." Bloodied lips struggle to form the word. "Father . . . into your hands I give my spirit."

Without warning, his body twists upward, enabling him to inhale sharply. The final words of Yeshua rip across the landscape like a lion's roar.

"It . . .

. . . is . . .

. . . accomplished!"

His head slumps forward against his chest.

Silence sweeps the Hill of the Skull.

Miryam feels her legs pulling her up the slope. She is running. At the crest of the hill, she collapses, pummeling the wooden stake with her fists as she tumbles to the ground. Her fingertips rake and gouge the moist earth.

No words can express her sorrow. No tears are left to drown it. All that remains is utter, aching emptiness. She lies in the dirt, heaving, unable to move. At last, a mantle falls gently across her shoulders, and tender hands lift her to her feet. "Mother," she hears a distant murmur, "my dear mother, it's your son, Yochanan. Let's go home."

HOLINESS IN THE MIDST OF UNHOLINESS

In the opening scene of the film *La Dolce Vita*,[4] a helicopter hovers above the meadows of central Italy. The statue of a man swings gently beneath the helicopter. His arms are open wide, as if he longs to embrace the lush landscape that passes underneath his feet. His head is slightly bowed, as if he is preparing to pray. The helicopter drifts across a freshly plowed field and several farmers recognize the robed figure.

"Jesus!" one farmhand cries. "It's Jesus!"

When the helicopter reaches the outskirts of Rome, the pilot glimpses several bikini beauties relaxing beside a pool. The helicopter circles abruptly and hovers above the pool. The workers in the aircraft strain to look past the statue, to gain a better view of the scantily clad women beneath them.

For a few moments, the Messiah hovers above the pool, arms outspread and head bowed. The sacred statue seems strangely out of place. He doesn't belong here. And yet, here he is—an unexpected outburst of holiness in the midst of an unholy event.

The same could be said for the prayers that Yeshua prayed from the stake of execution. They were unexpected outbursts of holiness in the midst of human unholiness. These prayers were as out of place on an execution-stake as was the statue of the Messiah dangling above the shapely citizens of some picturesque Italian suburb.

Yeshua wasn't the first revolutionary that the Roman soldiers had hammered to the splintered crossbeams. The soldiers knew precisely what to expect from this brand of criminal. Before the ill-fated Galilean lapsed into delirium, he would probably cry out to his God. One prayer would be a curse upon his executioners; the other would be a confession of his own sins.

But this wonder-working radical from Nazareth was different from the others.

Instead of the curse, he requested forgiveness—not for himself but for the soldiers who had spat upon him, for the bystanders who mocked him, for the centurion whose cold spear would find its way into his side. And instead of a confession, he begged heaven for an answer. Heaven never yielded an audible reply, but that didn't stop a centurion from whispering, "Surely, this man was innocent" (Luke 23:47). Never before had he encountered a man like this—a man who never cursed, who never confessed, and who never gave up.

THE FIRST PRAYER: THE PLEA OF FORGIVENESS

Let's be brutally honest for a moment: Cursing can bring a sense of satisfaction. I don't mean using colorful language. By "cursing," I mean asking God to give someone what he deserves. The whole idea is a bit self-righteous—after all, if God gave everyone what she or he deserved, I wouldn't be around to write these words and you wouldn't have survived long enough to read them. And yet, this sort of cursing appears throughout the Hebrew Scriptures.

King David pleaded regarding his enemies, "When they attack, let them be put to shame!" (Ps. 109:28). Jeremiah, the so-called weeping prophet, seems to have spent more time cursing than he did crying. "Take vengeance for me on my persecutors," he prayed once. "Let my persecutors be ashamed, not me; let them be terrified, not me. Bring on them the day of disaster, destroy them with double destruction" (Jer. 15:15; 17:18). When King Joash's minions murdered one of his priests, the priest bellowed, "May ADONAI see this and take vengeance!" (2 Chron. 24:22).

The soldiers around the execution-stake expected this self-proclaimed Messiah to follow in this tradition. After all, curses were what they had heard from other rabble-rousers. And it wasn't as if Yeshua hadn't cursed anyone before—religious leaders, fig trees, entire cities. Yeshua had even cursed one of his own followers: "The Son of Man will die just as the *Tanakh* says he will; but woe to that man by whom the Son of Man is betrayed! It would have been better for him had he never been born!" (Matt. 26:24).

Yet, hanging from the stake, Yeshua cursed no one. Not the *talmidim* who had high-tailed it out of the garden as soon as they saw the warrant for their teacher's arrest. Not the soldiers who had found amusement in the beating of a helpless prisoner. Not even the auxiliary who had hammered a spike through his wrist. Why? Paul recorded the answer: "The Messiah redeemed us from the curse pronounced in the *Torah* by becoming cursed on our behalf.'" (Gal. 3:13).

Why didn't the crucified Messiah curse anyone?

Because on the stake of execution, he *became* cursed.

He did not curse because he *was* the curse.

Yeshua could not scream at the sneering spectators, "Bring on them the day of disaster, destroy them with double destruction!"—the destruction of their sin was already consuming his own inmost being. He could not cry to the Roman auxiliaries, "Woe to you!"—his own soul was already choking on the woe of their sin. He could not even whisper, "Oh Lord, put my enemies to shame"—for in that moment, he *became* the enemy of God. At the intersection of those two wooden beams, Yeshua did not merely bear the pain of God's punishment for sin—he *became* the pain, the shame, the curse of humanity's sin.

That's why the soldiers never heard the curse that they anticipated. Instead, they heard an utterly unexpected outburst of holiness in the midst of this unholy event: "Father, forgive them; they don't understand what they are doing" (Luke 23:34). Yeshua could forgive them instead of cursing them because he had taken the curse of their sin and made it his own.

At times I would prefer to ignore this prayer. I don't know about the people who cross your path, but the people in my life sometimes deserve a curse or two in the tradition of David, Jeremiah, and Zechariah. I have met congregational leaders who are dishonest and youth who are disrespectful. The other drivers on the highway are disagreeable, and the waitress forgot to put a slice of lemon in my Diet Coke *again*. And me? Well, honestly, I'm no better than any of them. Yet, if I believe that Yeshua became the curse of God, I cannot pray, "Oh Lord, give them what they deserve." What I must pray instead is, "Father, forgive them. Maybe they know what they're doing, maybe they don't. It doesn't really matter. What matters is that your Son became the curse that they deserve. I bear nothing, for you have already borne it all." Hopefully, they are willing to say the same about me.

While cursing in the tradition of the prophets may seem more satisfying—at least for the first few moments—human curses will always ring hollow in the ears of those who have taken their stand in the shadow of the Hill of the Skull. So I forgive others, I love the youth, and I smile at the reckless cretin in the black SUV. And the waitress? I give her a twenty percent tip anyway. My redemption from sin occurred on an execution-stake, after all—not on a set of scales. If my redemption *did* depend on a set of scales, *I* would have been the one on the stake.

THE SECOND PRAYER: THE CRY FOR AN ANSWER

Decades of Jewish tradition had provided a prayer for nearly every life experience, from the washing of hands to the sighting of a rainbow. There was even a prayer for the experience of being executed. It was a simple plea: "May my death atone for all my sins."[5] The Roman soldiers had probably never seen a victim of this form of execution go to his grave without murmuring some such words to his deity.

Not until that day, during the *Pesach* festival. *That* day, when the Romans nailed the rabbi from Nazareth to the wooden beams. The Nazarene never prayed the prayer of confession. He could not, of course, because he had no sins to confess. Yet in that moment, Yeshua *was*, in some sense, sinful. According to Paul, "God made this sinless man be a sin offering on our behalf"—literally, "God caused the one who knew no sin to be sin" (2 Cor. 5:21). Paul did not write, "God caused him to bear sin" or even "to die for sin." No! God caused his Son "to *be* sin!" That is the horrible paradox of Yeshua's execution: On that day, the Sinless One became the sinfulness of all sinners, the vile essence of sin itself. In those moments, Yeshua

> becomes a bad man, the worst of all men, the badness, in fact, of all men and all women together . . . Between the third hour and the ninth hour, beneath a blackening sky,

[he] becomes the rebellion of humankind against its God. . . Yet [he] is also the Holy One of God . . . Holy, he must hate sin with an unyielding hatred. Behold, then, and see a sorrow unlike any other sorrow in the universe: that right now Jesus hates himself with unyielding hatred.[6]

In this way, God gains a ghastly new experience: Through the death of Yeshua, God experiences sin. Not the experience of committing sin. Not the fleeting rush of false satisfaction that seduces us into coming back for more. Not the feeble imitations of God's pleasure that the world foolishly calls pleasure. No, God experiences sin as it truly is: God experiences the decades of self-hatred that follow the fleeting rush of pleasure; God drinks down the darkest dregs of addiction and exploitation; God freely endures the eternal damnation for my flirtations with the boundaries of iniquity. Joni Eareckson Tada poignantly describes Yeshua's pain in these moments:

His Father! He must face his Father like this!
From heaven the Father now rouses himself like a lion disturbed, shakes his mane, and roars against the shriveling remnant of a man hanging on a cross: "Son of Man! Why have you behaved so? You have cheated, lusted, stolen, gossiped—murdered, envied, hated, lied . . . Oh, the duties you have shirked, the children you have abandoned! . . . What a self-righteous, pitiful drunk—*you*, who molest young boys, peddle killer drugs, travel in cliques, and mock your parents. . . . Does the list never end! Splitting families, raping virgins, acting smugly, playing the pimp—buying politicians, practicing extortion, filming pornography, accepting bribes . . . I hate, I *loathe* these things in you! Disgust for everything about you consumes me! Can you not feel my wrath?" The Father watches as his heart's treasure, the mirror-image of himself, sinks drowning into raw, liquid sin. [His] stored wrath against humankind from every century explodes in a single direction.

"My God! My God! Why have you forsaken me?"

But heaven stops its ears. The Son stares up at the One who cannot, who will not, reach down or reply. Two eternal hearts tear—their intimate relationship shaken to the depths.[7]

In the words of the prophet Isaiah,

"It was our diseases he bore, our pains from which he suffered; yet we regarded him as punished, stricken and afflicted by God. But he was wounded because of our crimes, crushed because of our sins; the disciplining that makes us whole fell on him, and by his bruises we are healed. We all, like sheep, went astray; we turned, each one, to his own way; yet ADONAI laid on him the guilt of all of us." (Isa. 53:4–6)

And nothing can ease his sorrow—not a prayer of confession, not the forgiveness of his Father, not even some sweet internal awareness that he is innocent. For in this moment, God's Son is sin. Yet he cannot confess his sinfulness, because his sin is not his own. This was "the cup"—the experience of God's wrath—that he begged his Father to let him bypass (Mark 14:36; see also Ps. 11:6; 75:8).

The crowd around the execution-stake expects a prayer of confession. What they hear instead of a confession is a cry of absolute agony: "My God! My God! Why have you deserted me?" Yeshua cannot beg, "Have mercy on me"—how can a holy God have mercy on the essence of sin? He cannot plead, "Father, forgive me"—of what sin can his Father forgive him? He can only pray for an answer—"My God! My God! Why have you deserted me?"

His cry is a quotation from Psalm 22. But screamed from the hill of Calvary, the prayer is no pious recitation of a Scripture passage. This is a cry of utter desperation. This is the cry of God's Son, utterly forsaken by his Father. In this cry, the face that Moses was forbidden to see (see Exod. 33:19–20) now finds itself turned toward the heavens, screaming for an answer.

This prayer is, I believe, the only adequate answer to the problems of pain and suffering in the world. It's an embarrassing answer, to be sure—after all, who wants to follow someone who allowed himself to get nailed to a stake of execution? Only a God who can identify with how it feels to dangle from an execution-stake can empathize with his people when their circumstances nail them to stakes of loneliness, loss, abandonment, persecution, and abuse. Such a God knows how it feels to be the victim. For, on the Hill of the Skull, he *chose* to become the victim.

This second prayer doesn't provide us with an escape from the problems of pain and suffering. It doesn't even provide us with answers to our questions of why. What it does provide is a reminder that we never suffer alone. And maybe, in the moments when we feel abandoned by God, that's the only answer we really need—which brings us to the third prayer that Yeshua prayed in the midst of his suffering.

THE THIRD PRAYER: THE WAY OF RUTHLESS TRUST

It is almost the ninth hour. The sun is beginning to peek through the clouds again. The priests on the Temple mount breathe a sigh of relief. They will be able to offer the evening sacrifices after all. The lambs, already slaughtered and flayed, dangle from wooden racks in the Court of Israel. As priests scurry to remove the carcasses from the iron hooks, the high priest lifts his arms and speaks the invocation for the evening sacrifice: "Into your hands I commit my spirit" (Ps. 31:5).[8]

At this moment, another man quotes the same Scripture: "Into your hands," he prays, "I commit my spirit." Through this prayer, prayed at this moment, Yeshua identifies himself as the *Pesach* sacrifice. Yet, what amazes me most about his prayer is the word that he adds to the quotation, "Father." God our Father has cursed him, forsaken him, and caused him to become the essence of sin, but Yeshua never gives up on his Father's love. He does not merely trust his Father; he trusts his Father with what Brennan Manning has termed *"ruthless trust."*

What is ruthless trust? It's refusing to give up on God's love for humanity, even when God seems to be playing on the wrong team. It's Jacob, putting God's messenger in a headlock and panting, "I won't let you go unless you bless me" (Gen. 32:26). It's Job crying out in the midst of his pain, "I know that my Redeemer lives" (Job 19:25). It's John, abandoned on the island of Patmos, still seeking the Spirit's presence (Rev. 1:1–8). It's the clergyman, giving the best years of his service in a congregation that has broken his heart, because that's where God has placed him. It's the new parents, standing over a pink-ruffled crib, praying, "Heal her or take her—we will still praise you." It's Yeshua *HaMashiach* gasping after six hours of agony, "Father, into your hands I commit my spirit."

> [Ruthless trust] inspires us to thank God for the spiritual darkness that envelops us, for the loss of income, for the nagging arthritis that is so painful, and to pray from the heart, "*Abba*, in your hands I entrust my body, mind, and spirit and this entire day.... Whatever you want of me, *I* want of me, falling into you and trusting you in the midst of my life. Into your heart, I entrust my heart, feeble, distracted, insecure, uncertain. *Abba*, unto you I abandon myself."[9]

The path of ruthless trust is a difficult path, to be sure. Yet, for those who follow the man executed between two thieves, it's the *only* path.

REFLECTIONS OF GOD'S HEART

Three prayers, spoken while staring into the face of death: The first a model of grace, the second a source of comfort, the last an example of trust. Each one a reflection of the heart of God. None of these prayers is easy to live. They require a lifestyle of forgiveness, brokenness, and ruthless trust. Yet, for those who take their stand in the shadow of Golgotha, they are the words that lead to life.

A MEDITATION

Lord of creation, Lord of life,
The folks around your feet expected a curse—
it's what I would have expected too.
I would have told the whole lot of them to go to hell.
But you forgave them—you *forgave* them!—
to teach us that we can do better
than giving people what they deserve.
We can give them mercy.
This is your grace.

The folks around your feet expected a confession—
it's what I would have expected too.
Was there really absolutely nothing that you regretted?

But you cried for an answer.
To teach us that because you became sin,
we will never suffer alone again.
God suffers with us.
This is our comfort.

The folks around your feet expected you to give up
on your Father—
it's what I would have expected too.
Whenever my way becomes painful, I want to give up.
But you still called God "Father"—why did you do it?
To teach us the way of ruthless trust in a heavenly Father
who will never let us go.
This is your promise.

Please show me how to share this grace,
to embrace this comfort,
to trust your promise.

Chapter Ten

Praying in the Shadow of a Shining Face—
Creating a New Future in the Glory of
God's Blessing

THE PRIESTLY BLESSING

Adonai said to Moshe [Moses], "Speak to Aharon [Aaron] and his sons, and tell them that this is how you are to bless the people of Isra'el: you are to say to them,

'*Y'varekh'kha* ADONAI *v'yishmerekha.*
[May ADONAI bless you and keep you.]
Ya'er ADONAI *panav eleikha vichunekha.*
[May ADONAI make his face shine on you and show you his favor.]
Yissa ADONAI *panav eleikha v'yasem l'kha shalom.*
[May ADONAI lift up his face toward you and give you peace.]'

In this way they are to put my name on the people of Isra'el, so that I will bless them." (Num. 6:22–27)

He led them out toward Beit-Anyah [Bethany]; then, raising his hands, he said a *b'rakhah* [blessing] over them; and as he was blessing them, he withdrew from them and was carried up into heaven. They bowed in worship to him, then returned to Yerushalayim, [Jerusalem] overflowing with joy. And they spent all their time in the Temple courts, praising God. (Luke 24:50–53)

No one—not even Yochanan—could keep up with him. The rabbi bounded up the eastern slope of the Kidron Valley toward the Mount of Olives. His feet were bare, and his hair whipped in the wind like the banner of a king.

His mother scurried up the hill, arm-in-arm with Miryam of Magdala. Joanna and Shlomit, Clopas and Miryam the mother of Ya'akov and Yochanan, relatives and friends—all of them trailed behind him, breathless with joy, and desperate never to let Yeshua out of their sight again.

They followed him through the groves of trees, past the stone olive-presses that surrounded the Gat Sh'manin (Garden of Gethsemane). The scents of spring swirled around them, strong and fresh in the morning air. Rays from the rising sun pierced the treetops and filled the grove with a thousand tiny shafts of light. Life seemed to erupt from the song of every sparrow, from the frightened leap of every hare, from the emerald hue of every blade of grass.

When Yeshua emerged from the trees on the eastern side of the Mount of Olives, he stopped abruptly. His followers gathered around him, and he began to embrace each of them.

When the teacher gripped Shim'on's shoulders, the big fisherman stiffened. His face burned with the shame of his denial, and his eyes brimmed with the guilt of his sin. He stared at the stones beneath his feet.

"Lord," Shim'on ventured, "is this the time when you will restore the kingdom of Isra'el?"

The rabbi chuckled, "The times and the periods that the Father has set by his power are not for any of you to know. Let me tell you about the power that is for you: The Holy Spirit will fall upon you, and you will testify about me in Jerusalem, in Judea and Samaria, even into the farthest reaches of the earth." [1]

Yeshua stepped away from the crowd and raised his hands. Behind him, the morning sun shone through the smoky pillars that drifted upward from newly kindled fires in the villages of Bethphage and Bethany. His mother closed her eyes in the glaring light.

When Yeshua spoke, it was not merely his voice that Miryam heard. A multitude of voices seemed to resound around him: "May ADONAI bless you and keep you. May ADONAI make his face shine on you and show you his favor. May ADONAI lift up his face toward . . . ."

Miryam didn't hear the final words of the benediction. She opened her eyes to look into her son's face, but the sun behind him had grown so bright—or was it the sun? She could see nothing but light, blinding light. For the briefest moment, she glimpsed the familiar outline of his body; then suddenly, she could not see him at all.

He was gone.

THE FINAL BLESSING

Forty days after the terror of the execution-stake and the triumph of the empty tomb, Yeshua's followers finally watched him ascend to his Father. For a few moments they stood, eyes wide and mouths sagging open, wondering what to do next. The duo of white-robed messengers didn't provide any help. "You Galileans!" they chided. "Why are you standing, staring into space? This Yeshua, who has been taken away from you into heaven, will come back to you in just the same way as you saw him go into heaven" (Acts 1:11).

Yes, but when? And how? The directions that Yeshua left were indefinite: "Stay here in the city until you have been equipped with power from above," he told them—but he never explained how they would know that their equipment had arrived (Luke 24:49). According to Luke, "as he was blessing them, he withdrew from them and was carried up into heaven" (Luke 24:51).

Ever feel like the first followers of Yeshua probably felt? Ever feel like God's presence has been whisked away into another realm? Like all that remains of his presence is the distant echo of his blessing? Don't despair—that distant echo of his blessing may be all that you need. It was, after all, all that his first followers needed. After Yeshua ascended, they "bowed in worship to him, then returned to Yerushalayim [Jerusalem], overflowing with joy. And they spent all their time in the Temple courts, praising God" (Luke 24:52–53).

Why were they able to leave the vacant spot where Yeshua had stood and dash into Jerusalem with psalms of joy ringing from their lips? I think it had to do with the blessing that he spoke as he was leaving.

THE PRIESTLY BENEDICTION

What blessing did Yeshua leave echoing in the ears of his first followers? No one can be certain, but it seems that Yeshua was speaking the ancient priestly benediction when his Father welcomed him home. Notice the resemblance between the description of Aaron's priestly benediction and Luke's account of Yeshua's final moments on this earth: Aaron "raised his hands toward the people, blessed them and came down" (Lev. 9:22). "Raising his hands, [Yeshua] said a *b'rakhah* [blessing] over them; and as he was blessing them, he . . . was carried up" (Luke 24:50–51).[2]

If Yeshua was conferring the priestly benediction, his blessing was a quotation from the book of Numbers. There, God had commanded Moses, "Speak to Aharon [Aaron] and his sons, and tell them that this is how you are to bless the people of Isra'el: you are to say to them, '*Y'varekh'kha* ADONAI *v'yishmerekha.* [May ADONAI bless you and keep you.] *Ya'er* ADONAI *panav eleikha vichunekha.* [May ADONAI make his face shine on you and show you his favor.] *Yissa* ADONAI *panav eleikha v'yasem l'kha shalom.* [May ADONAI lift up his face toward you and give you peace.]'" (Num. 6:22–27).

In the Hebrew Scriptures, these words had revealed the relationship that God desired to have with the Israelites. Through this benediction, God longed to reveal his grace—"make his face to shine"—among his people. That's why this benediction became a central part of Israel's worship. The priestly benediction echoed in the Temple after every act of obedience to the *Torah*, in the homes of Jewish children at the beginning of the Sabbath, in the Temple courts when Simeon blessed the infant Messiah. It was the blessing through which God imprinted his sacred identity on the Jewish people (see Num. 6:27). And when Yeshua vanished into the eastern horizon, the echoes of this benediction were all that remained.

THE EMBODIED BENEDICTION

The dozen *talmidim* that Yeshua had called to himself certainly didn't deserve the benediction. Six weeks earlier, on this same hill, they had scampered into the bushes when the soldiers showed up. During and after their rabbi's arrest, they deserted him, denied him, doubted him, and—except for a botched bit of swashbuckling swordplay, courtesy of Simon Peter—never once defended him. Yet in his final moments among them, Yeshua didn't say, "Remember what happened right over there, in the Garden of Gethsemane? Don't *ever* pull a stunt like that again!" Instead, in the very spot where this fickle band of followers had failed him, Yeshua asked his Father to bless them. Then, suddenly, he was gone.

And his followers?

They were a bit shocked, I suppose. Still, after Yeshua was gone, "they bowed to him." It was one thing to worship Yeshua while his feet were on the ground. But to bow to him after he was gone was to confess that, somehow, he was still present among them. They still didn't know *when* Yeshua would return. Neither did they know *how* they would get to the Father. But they did know—finally— *who* had revealed himself among them. They understood that the risen Messiah had not simply spoken the benediction. In Yeshua *HaMashiach*, the benediction of God became flesh.

In Yeshua *HaMashiach*, God *blessed* his people by giving them the gift of himself. He *kept* those who loved him by imprinting his own identity upon their lives (see John 17:11–12). He *shined his face* upon his followers—not only by giving them his love,[3] but also by giving them a glimpse of his glory on the mountain, where his face "shone like the sun" (Matt. 17:2). And he gave *peace*—not peace like the world offers, but the perfect contentment, the *shalom*, of his own presence (see John 14:27). In Yeshua *HaMashiach*, the living God blessed his people, kept them, caused his countenance to shine favorably upon them, and offered them grace and peace—forever.

By the time Yeshua blessed his followers on the Mount of Olives, the people of Israel had heard the benediction for fifteen centuries. But only in Yeshua *HaMashiach* did anyone *become* the benediction. The benediction that he spoke was a reminder of the benediction that he was.

LIVING THE BENEDICTION

Dial my telephone number and after the fourth ring, here's what you used to hear before I had mercy on my friends and changed the message: "Hi! You've reached the home of Timothy and Rayann Jones. Even though God answers everyone who calls on him, we don't. So, leave your name and your number, and, who knows, maybe we'll call you back." (Actually, you heard a shrieking guitar solo before the message; I wanted to make certain that you *really* wanted to talk to me.)

Late one evening, I stumbled to the spare bedroom and saw the light blinking on the answering machine. One message. I stabbed at the play button. At first, nothing. Then someone cleared his throat and muttered, "Man, don't you get it? God don't answer either." *Click.* No name. No number. Only silence.

I never discovered the caller's identity, but I do know one thing: he felt like God had deserted him. In the language of the Hebrew Scriptures, he felt as if God had "hidden his face"—as if God's face no longer shined on him (see, for example, Deut. 31:17–20; Ps. 13:1; Ezek. 39:29). He felt as if the blessing of God was not for him.

Have you ever felt that way before? I have. I'm sure I'll feel that way again. But here's the good news—God's steadfast love for his children was settled once and for all through Yeshua's life, death, and resurrection. Because of the one who embodied the benediction of God, God's face never stops shining on his children—even when his children feel that they are in the dark. In the words of Paul, God "has made his light shine in our hearts, the light of the knowledge of God's glory shining in the face of the Messiah Yeshua" (2 Cor 4:6).

That's why, on the evening of Yeshua's return to his Father, his followers found themselves whooping it up in the Temple courts instead of moping around the Mount of Olives. They knew that God's face was shining upon them, even when Yeshua was no longer beside them.

Of course, the shining face of God is no guarantee that our lives will be any easier. According to tradition, all but two of Yeshua's twelve *talmidim* died as martyrs. What the shining face of God *does* guarantee is that nothing in all of creation can remove God's favor from the lives of his children.

What does that mean in your day-by-day life? It means that your children may rebel against you and your sewer lines may rupture beneath you. Your house may collapse around you, and your spirit may cry out within you. And yet, God's face will never stop shining upon you. You can't earn his shining face, and you can't exploit it. You can only embrace it by receiving the one whose face still shines "like the sun in full strength" (Rev. 1:16).

A MEDITATION

The shining face of God . . .
the face that Moses could not see
the face that sent prophets to their knees
the face that speaks from eternity
That face was present in this man from Galilee.
Oh shining face of God,
please shine on me.

In the beginning was the Word, and the Word was with God, and the Word was God. He was with God in the beginning. . . . The Word became a human being and lived with us, and we saw his *Sh'khinah* [manifest glory of God], the *Sh'khinah* of the Father's only Son, full of grace and truth. No one has ever seen God; but the only and unique Son, who is identical with God and is at the Father's side—he has made him known. (John 1:1–2, 14, 18)

In the beginning, there was nothing. Nothing at all. Nothing but God. Only God. God and prayer.

Before the world came into being, the Father, Son, and Spirit lived in infinite, intimate fellowship with one another (see John 17). What is prayer if not intimate fellowship with God? And what is the glory of God if not the splendor of this intimate fellowship?[1]

A word arose within this intimate fellowship and spawned a single pinpoint of infinite destiny. Suns and spheres appeared, swirling, twirling in an eternal dance. Peaks and plains exploded through seething oceans. On one tiny patch of earth, the hopes and dreams of the cosmos converged around a man, a woman, and a pair of trees. The fellowship of the first couple was a living reflection of the glorious fellowship of God (see Gen. 1:26–27). And it was very good.

Then something unexplainable pierced the glory of God's good creation. Suddenly, all that had been so good became twisted into sin and sorrow and darkness and death. The specter of human selfishness engulfed the cosmos until only the dimmest reflections of glory remained.

In time, somewhere in the midst of that darkness a glimmer of glory arose again—"the true light, which gives light to everyone" (John 1:9).

This time, it was not merely a reflection of God's glory that pierced the formless void. This time, the living God personally pierced the sinews of time and space.

Only a band of scruffy shepherds heard the first prayer of praise recorded after the arrival of Messiah, God's glory: "In the

122

Afterword

highest heaven, glory to God! And on earth, peace among people of good will" (Luke 2:14).

Glory . . . the dazzling splendor of God's presence, veiled in human flesh. Glory . . . not on the wings of angels but in the womb of a teenaged peasant. Glory . . . not on a cushion beside the crackling logs of a fireplace, but in a feed-trough amid the steaming dung of sheep and goats.

Yochanan described Yeshua's glory with this phrase: It was "the Sh'khinah of the Father's only Son, full of grace and truth" (John 1:14). Yeshua's glory was not his dazzling beauty and splendor—his glory was his status as his Father's only Son.

How did Yeshua sustain this glorious fellowship? "Very early in the morning, while it was still dark, Yeshua got up, left, went away to a lonely spot and stayed there praying"; the verb tense in this sentence suggests that this was Yeshua's consistent habit (Mark 1:35). Even in the dark shadow of the execution-stake, he prayed, "Father, glorify your name!" (John 12:28).

Through the prayers of the Jew, Jesus we are able to glimpse the inner life of God. We see...

. . . a God who delights in doing the unexpected.

. . . a God who shatters our assumptions about his works and his ways.

. . . a God who desires to create a community that reflects his glory.

. . . a God who longs so deeply for a new future for us that he was willing to sacrifice his Son to create it.

And that's not all. Just as importantly, the prayers Yeshua prayed reveal that, at the center of God's being, there is a glorious fellowship of prayer. That means that, when we pray, we are not merely sending a few sentences to the ruler of the universe—though that would be amazing enough by itself. Through prayer, we "share in God's nature" (2 Pet. 1:4). We experience the infinite, inner fellowship of God. We receive a foretaste of the glorious future that God has planned for us.

Karl Barth once commented, "To clasp hands in prayer is the beginning of an uprising against the disorder of the world." [2] I think he was right. When I pray, I participate in the inner life of the One who longs to see his creation perfectly reflect his own glory, and who was willing to sacrifice the Jew, Jesus, his precious Messiah, to see his longing fulfilled.

ENDNOTES

CHAPTER ONE

[1] Leviticus 1:14–17; 5:7–10. See Walter C. Kaiser, Jr., "Leviticus," in *New Interpreter's Bible* vol. 1 (Nashville: Abingdon, 1994), 1013–14.

[2] A few scholars believe that Yeshua was not redeemed and therefore remained the special property of God. See Bo Reicke, "Jesus, Simeon, and Anna," in *Saved by Hope*, ed. J.I. Cook (Grand Rapids: Eerdmans, 1978), 100, and Charles H. Talbert *Reading Luke* (New York: Crossroad, 1992), 36–38. While this hypothesis might make sense theologically, it does not fit the biblical text. Choosing not to redeem a firstborn child does not fit with Luke's descriptive clause "to do what the *Torah* required" (Luke 2:27; cf. Exod. 13:13; Num. 18:15).

[3] Exodus 13:2; Numbers 18:15–16.

[4] This reconstruction of the liturgy for the redemption of firstborn sons is adapted from A.Z. Idelsohn, *Jewish Liturgy and Its Development* (New York: Schocken, 1962), 167–68, and A. Millgram, *Jewish Worship* (Philadelphia: Jewish Publication Society, 1971), 323–24.

[5] Numbers 6:23–25

[6] Jewish people in the first half of the first century may have prayed the *Amidah* daily rather than weekly. However, the earliest reference of this practice stems from 80 C.E. (see the reference to Rabban Gamaliel II in M. Berakhoth 4:3). (References to *The Mishnah* [Philadelphia: Jewish Publication Society] are indicated by "m." followed by the tractate title, then section and verse numbers.)

[7] Not all recensions of the *Amidah* conclude with this plea. However, even if this prayer of expectation postdates Yeshua's earthly ministry, it still expresses the essential Messianic expectations of first-century Jewish faith.

[8] Moshe Ben-Maimon, *Mishneh Torah, Sefer Shoftim, Hilchot Melachim U'Milchamoteihem*, 11. Although Moshe Ben-Maimon was a medieval rabbi, the lines quoted here probably reflect earlier Jewish Messianic expectations. I have excluded some lines included by Ben-Maimon which seem to be responses to the destruction of the Jewish Temple in 70 C.E. and to the presence of persons who had embraced Yeshua as the Messiah in the Jewish community.

[9] Reconstructed from Dead Sea Scroll fragment 1Q34:5:1.

[10] The language used here echoes the Messianic prophecies of Isaiah 52:7–10.

[11] Frederick Buechner, *The Hungering Dark* (New York: HarperSanFrancisco, 1985), 14.

CHAPTER TWO

[1] *Hallel* means "praise." These songs of praise comprise Psalms 113–118.

[2] See Matthew 13:55

[3] *Tzitziyot* are specially made fringes worn on the four corners of a man's garment, according to Numbers 15:37–41. *T'fillin* are small leather boxes (also known as *phylacteries*), which Jewish males tied to their hands and to their foreheads, in accordance with Deuteronomy 6:8. Also see glossary.

[4] Today, a Jewish male becomes a "son of the commandment" (*bar mitzvah*) when he reaches thirteen—a practice that was not widespread until the fifteenth century A.D. When a Jewish male turned twelve in the first century C.E., he "would be in Jewish terms beginning to make the transition into adult responsibility under the law" (J. Nolland, *Luke 1:1–9:20* in *Word Biblical Commentary* vol. 35a [Dallas: Word 1989], 129). "At the age of twelve the instruction of boys became more intensive in preparation of the recognition of adulthood" (D.L. Bock, *Luke* [Grand Rapids: Zondervan, 1996], 99).

[5] Cf. Deuteronomy 30:11–14. Prophets and rabbis frequently referred to *Torah* as a "yoke" (cf., e.g., Jer. 2:20; 5:5; see also Acts 15:10; Gal. 5:1). When Yeshua said that his "yoke was easy" (Matt. 11:29–30), he used a popular depiction of the *Torah* to identify himself as one who, as the incarnation of God's Word (John 1:1), filled the *Torah* with meaning.

[6] Cf. A. Millgram, *Jewish Worship* (Philadelphia: Jewish Publication Society, 1971), 96–101. The *Sh'ma* is the central expression of the Jewish faith. The Hebrew word *Sh'ma* means "hear" or "obey." It is drawn from the opening clause of Deuteronomy 6:4. In the first century, the recitation of the *Sh'ma* probably consisted of a blessing, three Scripture passages, and another blessing. The Scriptures were Deuteronomy 6:4–9; Deuteronomy 11:13–21; and Numbers 15:37–41. For sake of brevity, I have condensed the Scripture passages.

[7] The word *bless* is the most frequent English translation of the Hebrew word *barukh* and of the Greek verb *eulogeo*.

[8] A. Millgram, *Jewish Worship* (Philadelphia: Jewish Publication Society, 1971), 96–101.

[9] Notice the connection between blessedness and God's name in Exodus 20:24; Numbers 6:27; and, Psalm 63:4.

[10] Joni Eareckson Tada and Steve Estes, *When God Weeps: Why Our Sufferings Matter to the Almighty* (Grand Rapids: Zondervan, 1997), 45.

[11] Philip Yancey, *The Jesus I Never Knew* (Grand Rapids: Zondervan, 1995), 36.

[12] Thomas Cahill, *Desire of the Everlasting Hills* (New York: Doubleday, 1999), 89.

[13] Brennan Manning, *The Ragamuffin Gospel* rev. ed. (Sisters, Oregon: Multnomah, 2000), 167.

[14] Some phrases in this prayer were drawn from Ken Taylor, *Praying the Passion: Daily Readings and Prayers for Lent* (Nashville, Tennessee: Abingdon, 2000), 21.

CHAPTER THREE

[1] Luke 3:14.

[2] One "stadium" equaled the distance of a race in a Roman stadium, roughly one-fifth of a kilometer. Biblical scholars are uncertain of the exact location of Cana. The location described here—fifteen kilometers north of Nazareth, approximately halfway between the Sea of Galilee and the Mediterranean Sea—appears to me to be the most probable suggestion.

[3] Cf. 3 Maccabees 4:6. Ten silver coins seem to have constituted the minimum dowry that the *ketubah* (marriage contract) guaranteed the bride. This dowry remained hers, even if the marriage was dissolved (cf. Craig S. Keener's comments in *The IVP Bible Background Commentary: New Testament* [Downers Grove, Illinois: Intervarsity, 1993], 232). The coins would have been drachmae or denarii. Each coin was worth approximately one day's wages. According to some reconstructions, first-century women wore the ten coins in a crown. The authenticity of this tradition is uncertain, but it is certainly plausible. Luke 15:8 could refer to this custom.

[4] Cf. Isaiah 61:10; 3 Maccabees 4:8. This declaration in found in the Elephantine papyri. In contemporary Judaism, the betrothal (*eyrusin*) and the wedding (*nissuin*) occur in the same ceremony. In the first century, the betrothal usually took place several months before the wedding, although it could occur immediately before the wedding (cf. Tobit 7:21–8:1).

[5] Natan'el was from Cana (John 21:2) and seems to have been Yeshua's only connection to Cana. ("Simon the Cananean" was *not* from Cana; "Cananean" is a poor transliteration of the Aramaic word for "Zealot.") Therefore, in the context of John 1:43–2:11, it is possible that the wedding was for a relative or close friend of Natan'el and that Yeshua, his mother Miryam, and the disciples attended the feast as Natan'el's guests. In the other Gospels, Natan'el is called "Bartholomew" (literally, "Bar-Tolmai"), which means "Tolmai's son."

[6] Galena is a form of lead. In the ancient world, powdered galena was often used as eye-shadow.

[7] Luke 1:33.

[8] It is difficult to reconstruct the wedding blessings that would have been used around 30 C.E. After the destruction of the Jewish Temple, additional lines were inserted into the blessings, asking God to restore joy and gladness to Jerusalem. I have adapted this reconstruction from several rabbinic tractates and from A. Millgram, *Jewish Worship* (Philadelphia: Jewish

Publication Society, 1971), 328–29; A.Z. Idelsohn, *Jewish Liturgy and Its Development* (New York: Schocken, 1960), 169–70; R. Posner, et al., *Jewish Liturgy* (Jerusalem: Keter, 1975), 238.

⁹ Blaise Pascal, *Pensees*, 425.

¹⁰ In terms of frequency, the depiction of God as Israel's lover (Isa. 54:1–7; 62:4–5; Jer. 2:2; 2:29–32; 3:20; 31:32; Ezek. 16:1–63; 23:1–49; Hosea 2:1–3:5) is second only to the image of God as the sovereign king (Isa. 6:5; 33:17–22; 41:21; 43:15; 44:6; Jer. 10:6–10; 46:18; 48:15; 51:57; Ezek. 20:33; Dan. 4:37; Zeph. 3:15; Zech. 14:9–19; Mal. 1:14).

¹¹ Cf. Leonard I. Sweet, *SoulTsunami: Sink or Swim in New Millennium Culture* (Grand Rapids: Zondervan, 1999), 423. For the ancient Hebrews' view of sexual pleasure, see, e.g., Song of Solomon 1, 4–7; Tobit 8:4–9.

¹² Manning, *The Ragamuffin Gospel* rev. ed., 88–89.

¹³ Carol Memmott, "Buy into Hilarious 'Shopaholic' Binge," review of Sophie Kinsella, *Confessions of a Shopaholic,* in *USA Today,* 15 February 2001, sec. 4D

¹⁴ Walter Burkhardt, *Still Proclaiming Your Wonders* (Mahwah, New Jersey: Paulist, 1984), 168.

¹⁵ In the gospel of John, the first event at which Yeshua reveals his identity is a wedding. So is the last. The final event in the book of Revelation is the marriage of the Messiah to his people (Rev. 19–22).

¹⁶ Brennan Manning, *Lion and Lamb: The Relentless Tenderness of Jesus* (Grand Rapids: Chosen, 1986), 58, 90.

¹⁷ Some portions of this prayer are drawn from the benediction in Manning, *Lion and Lamb,* 124–25.

CHAPTER FOUR

¹ Matthew 23:6; Luke 11:43.

² Prayers in this chapter are drawn from the rabbinic sources quoted in these texts: C.W. Dugmore, *The Influence of the Synagogue Upon the Divine Office* (Oxford: Oxford University, 1944) 115–24; E. Ferguson, *Backgrounds of Early Christianity* 2ⁿᵈ ed. (Grand Rapids: Eerdmans, 1993) 539–46; Emil Schurer, *The History of the Jewish People in the Age of Jesus Christ* repr., ed. G. Vermes, et al. (Edinburgh: T&T Clark, 1979) 2:456–61.

³ Lawrence A. Hoffman, ed., *My People's Prayer Book, Vol. 2: Traditional Prayers, Modern Commentaries—The Amidah* (Woodstock, VT: Jewish Lights, 1998) 152–84.

⁴ Luke 4:18–19. The reading is a paraphrase of Isaiah 61:1–2 with the words "and a day of vengeance" omitted and a phrase from Isaiah 58:6 added.

⁵ C.S. Lewis, *The Lion, the Witch, and the Wardrobe* (New York: Macmillan, 1950) 75–76.

⁶ Elie Wiesel, *Twilight* (New York: Warner, 1987) 207.

⁷ C.J.H. Wright, *Knowing Jesus through the Old Testament,* as quoted in Philip Yancey, *The Bible Jesus Read* (Grand Rapids: Zondervan, 1999) 185–86.

8 Eugene Peterson, *A Long Obedience in the Same Direction* (Downers Grove, Illinois: InterVarsity, 1980) 190.
9 C.S. Lewis, *The Weight of Glory and Other Addresses* (Grand Rapids: Eerdmans, 1965) 1–2.
10 Friedrich Buechner, *Wishful Thinking* rev. ed. (New York: HarperCollins, 1993) 87.

CHAPTER FIVE

1 Kaddish is an Aramaic word meaning "holy." This traditional prayer recognizes the holiness of God's name. It is prayed in synagogue services, at funerals, at memorial services, and at other special times.
2 Paraphrased from *The Union Prayerbook for Jewish Worship* rev. ed. (Cincinnati: CCAR, 1948), 342.
3 Robert Guelich, *The Sermon on the Mount* (Dallas: Word, 1982), 313; E. Moore, "Lead Us Not Into Temptation," *Expository Times* 102 (1991): 171–72.
4 Galilean Jews, who rarely sailed on large ships, referred to the Sea of Galilee as a "sea." It is more precisely, a lake. Roman soldiers, for whom sailing the Mediterranean Sea was a way of a life, scornfully called the Sea of Galilee "the pond."
5 The Gospels imply that when Yeshua began performing miracles, the crowds around him grew rapidly (cf. Matt. 4:23–25; Luke 5:12–15). When Yeshua refused to do miracles at the people's request, the crowds diminished (John 6:25–34, 60–66).
6 During his Galilean ministry, Yeshua seems to have stayed at Simon's home in Capernaum (Matt. 4:13; Mark 1:21, 29–33; 2:1–3; 9:33).
7 Although "blessed" is the rendering of *makarios* utilized here, "congratulations" might capture the word's meaning more accurately. *Makarios* is the Greek equivalent of the Hebrew root-word *ashr*, which means, "contented," "cheerful," "gifted," "congratulation," even "happy-go-lucky." (The translators of the French New Testament were on the right track when they rendered Matthew's third Beatitude, "Cheerful are the debonair".) The meaning that the English term "blessed" properly reflects is expressed through the Hebrew root-word *brkh* ("blessed," "bowed to") and its Greek equivalent *eulogetes* ("blessed," "thanked") (see, e.g., Luke 6:28). Although the meanings of *brkh*, *eulogetes*, and "blessed" overlap with *ashr*, *makarios* and "congratulations," the two word groups are not synonymous. Cf. G. Bettram, *"makarios,"* in *Theologisches Worterbuch Neuen testament* vol. 4, ed. G. Kittel (Stuttgart: Kohlhammer Verlag, 1964); H.W. Beyer, *"eulogetein,"* in *Theologisches Worterbuch neuen Testament* vol. 2; Charles Talbert, *Reading Luke* (New York: Crossroad, 1992), 72.
8 The Sermon on the Mount (Matt. 5–7) and the Sermon on the Plain (Luke 6:20–49) seem to be variations of a message that Yeshua preached in several ways in several places (see discussion in Guelich, 35; Nolland, 283–87). This reconstruction includes portions from each sermon.

[9] Portions of this paragraph allude to "A Peace of the Rock," *Preaching* (July–August 1995), 43–44.

[10] Manning, *The Ragamuffin Gospel* rev. ed., 28, 55.

[11] B. Nicholas, et al., "*patria potestas*," in *The Oxford Classical Dictionary*, ed. Simon Hornblower and Anthony Spawforth (Oxford: Oxford University Press, 1996), 1122–123.

[12] Quoted in Simon Tugwell, *The Beatitudes* (Springfield, Illinois: Templegate, 1980), 138.

[13] Walter Wangerin, Jr., *Reliving the Passion* (Grand Rapids: Zondervan, 1992), 66.

[14] Frederick Buechner, *Listening to Your Life*, as quoted in William Willimon and Stanley Hauerwas, *Lord, Teach Us: The Lord's Prayer and the Christian Life* (Nashville: Abingdon, 1996), 9.

CHAPTER SIX

[1] See chapter five, endnote 1.

[2] See M. Kethub. 4:4. Women were frequently hired to mourn a deceased person's death for thirty days. A family such as Lazarus' might also have hired flutists to play somber dirges during this time. See Ben Witherington III, *Women in the Ministry of Jesus: A Study of Jesus' Attitude Toward Women and their Roles as Reflected in his Earthly Life* (Cambridge: Cambridge University, 1984), 74–75.

[3] M. Kethub. 8.

[4] Quoted in Philip Yancey, *The Bible Jesus Read* (Grand Rapids: Zondervan, 1999), 35.

[5] Mark Buchanan, "Jesus Wept," in *Christianity Today*, 5 March 2001, 68.

CHAPTER SEVEN

[1] Language alludes to William Willimon and Stanley Hauerwas, *Lord, Teach Us: The Lord's Prayer and the Christian Life* (Nashville: Abingdon, 1996), 17, 21, 28.

[2] The modern Passover *seder* includes a fourth question and response about reclining at table. However, as this was added to the service after the Temple was destroyed, it would not have been part of the the the liturgy in Yeshua's day.

[3] Reconstruction based on M. Pesahim 10:1–9; Deuteronomy 26:5–8; R. Alan Culpepper, "Luke," in *New Interpreter's Bible* vol. 7 (Nashville: Abingdon, 1995), 418–19; Joachim Jeremias, *The Eucharistic Words of Jesus* (Philadelphia: Fortress, 1966), 84–88; and Anthony J. Saldarini, *Jesus and Passover* (Ramsey, New Jersey: Paulist, 1984), 32–50.

[4] The participants in the Exodus had to leave Egypt quickly. Roasted meat and unleavened bread could be prepared more quickly than boiled meat and leavened bread. Therefore, roasted meat and unleavened bread became the

symbols of their deliverance from Egypt. Boiled meat was preferred in the ancient world, because meat roasted over an open fire tended to be tough.

[5] For the sake of brevity, the *Pesach seder* has been condensed.

[6] I have included only selected portions of the *hallel* (Psalms 113–118). In a complete Seder, Psalms 113 and 114 would have been chanted in their entirety at this point.

[7] This was the second of four cups that the followers of Yeshua drank during the *Pesach* meal. After Yeshua drank from the first cup, he said, "I tell you that from now on, I will not drink the 'fruit of the vine' until the Kingdom of God comes" (Luke 22:18). He repeated the vow when he served the third cup (Matt. 26:29; Mark 14:25).

[8] The "giving thanks" mentioned in Luke 22:19 and 1 Corinthians 11:24 would have included the *Birkat HaMazon.*

[9] See Revelation 21, where the people of God are identified as the holy city.

CHAPTER EIGHT

[1] Culpepper, 462.

[2] Willimon and Hauerwas, 29.

[3] Quoted in James Bryan Smith, *Rich Mullins: An Arrow Pointing to Heaven* (Nashville: Broadman and Holman, 2000), 33.

CHAPTER NINE

[1] The Romans viewed the sun's absence as a sign of the death of a divine ruler. The poet Virgil wrote regarding Ceasar's death: "The sun shall give you signs. (Who would daresay that the sun might lie?) . . . After the Caesar sank from sight, he wrapped his face in darkened gloom, and a godless generation feared endless night." (Virgil, *Georgics,* in Loeb Classical Library [Cambridge: Harvard, 1978], 1:113.)

[2] According to Roman practice, the friends and family of the condemned person had to stand at a distance from the execution-stake, to prevent rescue attempts. In extremely rare circumstances, persons *were* rescued from stakes of execution, after friends overpowered, begged, or bribed guards. The trauma of a Roman execution was, however, so severe that survival was rare. The Jewish historian Josephus rescued three friends from execution-stakes. Only one survived. See Josephus, *Vita,* 420.

[3] The wine was *posca,* the diluted drink which quenched the thirst of Roman soldiers while allowing their senses to remain sharp. Yeshua appears to have drunk the *posca* so that his life could end with a cry of triumph. The wine that Yeshua refused on the way to his execution was strong wine, mingled with a drug to deaden the senses. According to the rabbis, "When one is led out to execution, he is given a cup of wine, containing frankincense, to numb his senses. . . . The noble women in Jerusalem used to donate it" (quoted in Leon Morris, *The Gospel According to John* [Grand Rapids: Eerdmans, 1971], 814).

⁴ La Dolce Vita. Dir. Federico Fellini. Koch Lorber, 1961.

⁵ See, e.g., Craig S. Keener, *The IVP Bible Background Commentary* (Downers Grove, Illinois: InterVarsity, 1993), 254.

⁶ Wangerin, 121–23.

⁷ Tada and Estes, 53–54.

⁸ The quotation from Psalm 31:5 was part of the liturgy for the evening sacrifice, offered at the ninth hour (Keener, 255).

⁹ Manning, *Ruthless Trust*, 11–12.

CHAPTER TEN

¹ Paraphrased from Acts 1:6–10.

² The language selected by Luke suggests an intentional parallel between Aaron's benediction and Yeshua's parting blessing (see, e.g., Joseph Fitzmyer, *The Gospel According to Luke, 10–24* [New York: Doubleday, 1985], 1590).

³ See, e.g., Psalm 31:16, where "let your face shine" implies God's steadfast love and salvation.

AFTERWORD

¹ Notice, in John 17:22, that the result of receiving God's glory is intimate fellowship.

² Quoted in Willimon and Hauerwas, 109.

Unless noted, all terms are of Hebrew origin.

Abba—Aramaic term for father. No precise English equivalent exists for this word which children and adults alike used to address their fathers. It is more intimate than "father," yet more reverent than "daddy."

Adonai—(Lord) Term for a divine ruler, used in the Hebrew Script-ures to refer to God. In prayers and in Scripture readings, *Adonai* frequently functioned as a substitute for the unspeakable holy name of God, YHVH, revealed to Moses at the burning bush (Exod. 3).

Amidah—(standing) Central prayer in the Jewish synagogue service. Also known as the *Shemoneh Esrei* ("Eighteen") because, by the Second Temple period, the late first century, the prayer included eighteen benedictions.

Aron Hakodesh—(holy ark) The chest in a synagogue in which the sacred scrolls of Scripture were kept. Also known as the *tebhah*.

bar—Aramaic for son.

bar mitzvah—Aramaic for "Son of the Commandment." The rite in which a Jewish male accepts his responsibility to learn and follow the *Torah*.

barukh—(bless) From the root *brkh*. "To bless" or "to bow the knee."

B.C.E. and C.E.—Respectively, these terms stand for "before the common era" (a Jewish alternative to B.C.) and "common era" (a Jewish alternative to A.D.).

Birkat HaMazon—(Grace after meals) The blessings recited after every meal that includes bread, based on Deuteronomy 8:10: "So you will eat and be satisified, and you will bless ADONAI, your God for the good land he has given you." The first-century form of the prayer included three parts—the *birkat hazan* (recognizing that God gives bread to the world), the *birkat ha'aretz* (thanking God for the land of Israel), and the *birkat Yerushalayim* (thanking God for Jerusalem and entreating God to send the Messiah).

b'rakhah (pl., *b'rakhot*)—(blessing) From the root *brkh*.

charoset—Mixture of fruit, nuts, and wine, eaten during the Passover celebration to remind Jews of the mortar that they made when they were slaves in Egypt. Yeshua probably dipped the bread that he handed to Judas into the *charoset* (John 13:26).

Elisheva—Elizabeth

eyrusin–betrothal

hallel—(Praise God) Usually refers to Psalms 113–118, through-out which praising God is a key theme.

heder—(Room or chamber) Place where the bride and groom consum-mated their marriage. Sometimes refers to a place of schooling.

huppah—(canopy) The canopy under which a Jewish bride and groom are married.

Kaddish—Aramaic for "holy." Prayer recognizing the holiness of God's name that is prayed in synagogue services, at funerals, at memorial services, and at other special times.

Kefa—Aramaic for "stone." Yeshua's nickname for his follower Simon. Equivalent to the Greek term *Petros,* from which the name "Peter" is derived.

Maror—(Bitter) Bitter herbs eaten during the Passover meal, to bring to mind the bitterness of the Israelites' slavery in Egypt.

Marta—Martha

Mashiach—(Messiah, anointed one) The redeemer of Israel, promised in the Hebrew Scriptures. "Christos" is the equivalent term in Greek.

matzah—Unleavened bread, traditionally served at Passover.

Miryam—Mary

Mishnah—Traditional interpretations and expansions of the Torah. The *Mishnah* remained an oral tradition until the second century C.E., when Rabbi Judah HaNasi compiled the oral traditions in written form. Together with the *gemara,* they are called the Talmud.

mitzvah, (pl., *mitzvot*)—A commandment given by God. A good deed.

Natan'el—Nathanael

nissuin—marriage

Pesach—(Passover) Celebration, beginning on the fourteenth of Nisan in the biblical calendar, celebrating the night when the angel of death passed over the houses of the Jewish people during their time of slavery in Egypt (see Exod. 12:13).

pidyon ha'ben—(redemption of the son) Release of a firstborn son from his responsibility to serve as a priest in the temple (see Num. 8:14–18).

rabbi—A teacher recognized as having the insight to make decis-ions on issues of Jewish law.

Ruach HaKodesh—the Holy Spirit, referred to only four times in the *Tanakh* as such, and many times as the Spirit of God.

seder—(order) Liturgical order followed when commemorating the *Pesach.*

Shabbat— Sabbath

shaliakh tzibbur—(messenger of the congregation) Individual chosen to expound the Scriptures in a synagogue service.

Shavu'ot—(Weeks) Celebration of the harvest of the firstfruits of the crops. It begins fifty days after the second day of the Passover festival. Also known as Pentecost or the Feast of Weeks.

sheva b'rakhot—(seven blessings) Blessings spoken at a Jewish wedding, recognizing God as the source and foundation of the couple's union.

Shim'on—Simeon, Simon

Sh'khinah—Divine presence. A rabbinic term, referring to the manifest glory of God dwelling among God's people.

Sh'ma—(hear) The central Jewish confession of faith, based on Deuteronomy 6:4–9.

shofar—ram's horn

synagogue—Greek for "assembly." Place designated for Jewish people to worship together and to study the Scriptures. Syna-gogues arose after the Babylonians destroyed the temple in 586 B.C.E. Even after the exile ended and the temple was rebuilt, synagogues continued to be central to Jewish religious life.

tallit—Fringed shawl, worn during the morning prayer service. The fringes were intended to fulfill the commandment of God found in Numbers 15:38. In ancient times, including the first century, the *tallit* was a cloak or robe included in normal male attire, to which *tzitziyot* were attached.

talmid (pl., *talmidim*)—Disciple, follower

Tanakh—Acronym formed from the first letters of the three parts of the Hebrew Bible—*Torah* ("Law," "Instruction"), *Nevi'im* ("Prophets"), and *K'tuvim* ("Writings"). Hence, the "Old" Testament. Rendered "Scripture" or "it is written" in most transla-tions of the New Testament.

tefillah—(discernment) General term for prayer. When capitalized, *Tefillah* refers to the *Amidah.*

t'fillin—Two black leather boxes containing scrolls with Bible passages on them (Exod. 13:1–16; Deut. 6:4–9; 11:13–21). During synagogue prayers, men affix one to their hand and arm and the other to the forehead, in obedience to Deuteronomy 6:8. *T'fillin* are called "phylacteries" in most translations (see Matt. 23:5).

Torah—(instruction) The first five books of the Hebrew Scriptures—Genesis, Exodus, Leviticus, Numbers, and Deuteronomy.

tzitzit (pl., *tzitziyot*)—Specially made fringes on the four corners of a man's garment in obedience to Numbers 15:37–41.

Ya'akov—Jacob, James

yeshu'ah—salvation

Yeshua—Hebrew name of Jesus, salvation

Yeshua HaMashiach—Jesus the Messiah

Yochanan—John

Yosef—Joseph

Z'kharyah—Zechariah

OTHER RELATED RESOURCES

Complete Jewish Bible: *A New English Version*

—Dr. David H. Stern

Presenting the Word of God as a unified Jewish book, the *Complete Jewish Bible* is a new version for Jews and non-Jews alike. It connects Jews with the Jewishness of the Messiah, and non-Jews with their Jewish roots. Names and key terms are returned to their original Hebrew and presented in easy-to-understand transliterations, enabling the reader to say them the way Yeshua (Jesus) did! 1697 pages.

Hardback	978-9653590151	**JB12**	$34.99
Paperback	978-9653590182	**JB13**	$29.99
Leather Cover	978-9653590199	**JB15**	$59.99
Large Print (12 Pt font)	978-1880226483	**JB16**	$49.99

Also available in French and Portuguese.

Jewish New Testament

—Dr. David H. Stern

The New Testament is a Jewish book, written by Jews, initially for Jews. Its central figure was a Jew. His followers were all Jews; yet no other version really communicates its original, essential Jewishness. Uses neutral terms and Hebrew names. Highlights Jewish references and corrects mistranslations. Freshly translated into English from Greek, this is a must read to learn about first-century faith. 436 pages.

Hardback	978-9653590069	**JB02**	$19.99
Paperback	978-9653590038	**JB01**	$14.99
Spanish	978-1936716272	**JB17**	$24.99

Also available in French, German, Polish, Portuguese and Russian.

Jewish New Testament Commentary

—Dr. David H. Stern

This companion to the *Jewish New Testament* enhances Bible study. Passages and expressions are explained in their original cultural context. 15 years of research. 960 pages.

Hardback	978-9653590083	**JB06**	$34.99
Paperback	978-9653590113	**JB10**	$29.99

Psalms & Proverbs *Tehillim* תְּהִלִּים-*Mishlei* מִשְׁלֵי

—Translated by Dr. David Stern

Contemplate the power in these words anytime, anywhere: Psalms-*Tehillim* offers uplifting words of praise and gratitude, keeping us focused with the right attitude; Proverbs-*Mishlei* gives us the wisdom for daily living, renewing our minds by leading us to examine our actions, to discern good from evil, and to decide freely to do the good. Makes a wonderful and meaningful gift. Softcover, 224 pages.

978-1936716692	LB90	$9.99

Messianic Judaism *A Modern Movement With an Ancient Past*
—David H. Stern

An updated discussion of the history, ideology, theology and program for Messianic Judaism. A challenge to both Jews and non-Jews who honor Yeshua to catch the vision of Messianic Judaism. 312 pages

978-1880226339   **LB62** $17.99

Restoring the Jewishness of the Gospel
A Message for Christians
—David H. Stern

Introduces Christians to the Jewish roots of their faith, challenges some conventional ideas, and raises some neglected questions: How are both the Jews and "the Church" God's people? Is the Law of Moses in force today? Filled with insight! Endorsed by Dr. Darrell L. Bock. 110 pages

English	978-1880226667	**LB70**	$9.99
Spanish	978-9653590175	**JB14**	$9.99

Come and Worship *Ways to Worship from the Hebrew Scriptures*
—Compiled by Barbara D. Malda

We were created to worship. God has graciously given us many ways to express our praise to him. Each way fits a different situation or moment in life, yet all are intended to bring honor and glory to him. When we believe that he is who he says he is [see *His Names are Wonderful!*] and that his Word is true, worship flows naturally from our hearts to his. Softcover, 128 pages.

978-1936716678   **LB88** $9.99

His Names Are Wonderful
Getting to Know God Through His Hebrew Names
—Elizabeth L. Vander Meulen and Barbara D. Malda

In Hebrew thought, names did more than identify people; they revealed their nature. God's identity is expressed not in one name, but in many. This book will help readers know God better as they uncover the truths in his Hebrew names. 160 pages.

978-1880226308   **LB58** $9.99

The Return of the Kosher Pig *The Divine Messiah in Jewish Thought*
—Rabbi Tzahi Shapira

The subject of Messiah fills many pages of rabbinic writings. Hidden in those pages is a little known concept that the Messiah has the same authority given to God. Based on the Scriptures and traditional rabbinic writings, this book shows the deity of Yeshua from a new perspective. You will see that the rabbis of old expected the Messiah to be divine. Softcover, 352 pages.

"One of the most interesting and learned tomes I have ever read. Contained within its pages is much with which I agree, some with which I disagree, and much about which I never thought. Rabbi Shapria's remarkable book cannot be ignored."

—Dr. Paige Patterson, President, Southwest Baptist Theological Seminary

978-1936716456   **LB81** $ 39.99

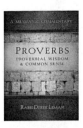

Proverbial Wisdom & Common Sense
A Messianic Commentary
—Derek Leman
A Messianic Jewish Approach to Today's Issues from the Proverbs
A devotional style commentary, divided into chapters suitable for daily reading. An encyclopedia of practical advice on topics relevant to everyone. 248 pages

Paperback	978-1880226780 **LB98**	$19.99

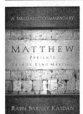

Matthew Presents Yeshua, King Messiah *A Messianic Commentary*
—Rabbi Barney Kasdan
Few commentators are able to truly present Yeshua in his Jewish context. Most don't understand his background, his family, even his religion, and consequently really don't understand who he truly is. This commentator is well versed with first-century Jewish practices and thought, as well as the historical and cultural setting of the day, and the 'traditions of the Elders' that Yeshua so often spoke about. Get to know Yeshua, the King, through the writing of another rabbi, Barney Kasdan. 448 pages

	978-1936716265 **LB76**	$29.99

Rabbi Paul Enlightens the Ephesians on Walking with Messiah Yeshua
A Messianic Commentary
—Rabbi Barney Kasdan
The Ephesian were a diverse group of Jews and Gentiles, united together in Messiah. They definitely had an impact on the first century world in which they lived. But the Rabbi was not just writing to that local group. What is Paul saying to us? 160 pages.

Paperback	978-11936716821 **LB99**	$17.99

James the Just Presents Application of Torah
A Messianic Commentary
—Dr. David Friedman
James (Jacob) one of the Epistles written to first century Jewish followers of Yeshua. Dr. David Friedman, a former Professor of the Israel Bible Institute has shed new light for Christians from this very important letter.

	978-1936716449 **LB82**	$14.99

Jude On Faith and the Destructive Influence of Heresy
A Messianic Commentary
—Rabbi Joshua Brumbach
Almost no other canonical book has been as neglected and overlooked as the Epistle of Jude. This little book may be small, but it has a big message that is even more relevant today as when it was originally written.

	978-1-936716-78-4 **LB97**	$14.99

At the Feet of Rabbi Gamaliel
Rabbinic Influence in Paul's Teachings
—David Friedman, Ph.D.

Paul (Shaul) was on the "fast track" to becoming a sage and Sanhedrin judge, describing himself as passionate for the Torah and the traditions of the fathers, typical for an aspiring Pharisee: "...trained at the feet of Gamaliel in every detail of the Torah of our forefathers. I was a zealot for God, as all of you are today" (Acts 22.3, CJB). Did Shaul's teachings reflect Rabbi Gamaliel's instructions? Did Paul continue to value the Torah and Pharisaic tradition? Did Paul create a 'New' Theology? The results of the research within these pages and its conclusion may surprise you. Softcover, 100 pages.

978-1936716753   LB95 $8.99

Debranding God *Revealing His True Essence*
—Eduardo Stein

The process of 'debranding' God is to remove all the labels and fads that prompt us to understand him as a supplier and ourselves as the most demanding of customers. Changing our perception of God also changes our perception of ourselves. In knowing who we are in relationship to God, we discover his, and our, true essence. Softcover, 252 pages.

978-1936716708   LB91 $16.99

Under the Fig Tree *Messianic Thought Through the Hebrew Calendar*
—Patrick Gabriel Lumbroso

Take a daily devotional journey into the Word of God through the Hebrew Calendar and the Biblical Feasts. Learn deeper meaning of the Scriptures through Hebraic thought. Beautifully written and a source for inspiration to draw closer to Adonai every day. Softcover, 407 pages.

978-1936716760   LB96 $25.99

Under the Vine *Messianic Thought Through the Hebrew Calendar*
—Patrick Gabriel Lumbroso

Journey daily through the Hebrew Calendar and Biblical Feasts into the B'rit Hadashah (New Testament) Scriptures as they are put in their rightful context, bringing Judaism alive in it's full beauty. Messianic faith was the motor and what gave substance to Abraham's new beliefs, hope to Job, trust to Isaac, vision to Jacob, resilience to Joseph, courage to David, wisdom to Solomon, knowledge to Daniel, and divine Messianic authority to Yeshua. Softcover, 412 pages.

978-1936716654   LB87 $25.99

The Revolt of Rabbi Morris Cohen
Exploring the Passion & Piety of a Modern-day Pharisee
—Anthony Cardinale

A brilliant school psychologist, Rabbi Morris Cohen went on a one-man strike to protest the systematic mislabeling of slow learning pupils as "Learning Disabled" (to extract special education money from the state). His disciplinary hearing, based on the transcript, is a hilarious read! This effusive, garrulous man with an irresistible sense of humor lost his job, but achieved a major historic victory causing the reform of the billion-dollar special education program. Enter into the mind of an eighth-generation Orthodox rabbi to see how he deals spiritually with the loss of everything, even the love of his children. This modern-day Pharisee discovered a trusted friend in the author (a born again believer in Jesus) with whom he could openly struggle over Rabbinic Judaism as well as the concept of Jesus (Yeshua) as Messiah. Softcover, 320 pages.

978-1936716722   **LB92** $19.99

Stories of Yeshua
—Jim Reimann, Illustrator Julia Filipone-Erez

Children's Bible Storybook with four stories about Yeshua (Jesus).
Yeshua is Born: The Bethlehem Story based on Lk 1:26-35 & 2:1-20; *Yeshua and Nicodemus in Jerusalem* based on Jn 3:1-16; *Yeshua Loves the Little Children of the World* based on Matthew 18:1–6 & 19:13–15; *Yeshua is Alive-The Empty Tomb in Jerusalem* based on Matthew 26:17-56, Jn 19:16-20:18, Lk 24:50-53. Ages 3-7, Softcover, 48 pages.

978-1936716685   **LB89** $14.99

To the Ends of the Earth – How the First Jewish Followers of Yeshua Transformed the Ancient World
— Dr. Jeffrey Seif

Everyone knows that the first followers of Yeshua were Jews, and that Christianity was very Jewish for the first 50 to 100 years. It's a known fact that there were many congregations made up mostly of Jews, although the false perception today is, that in the second century they disappeared. Dr. Seif reveals the truth of what happened to them and how these early Messianic Jews influenced and transformed the behavior of the known world at that time.

978-1936716463   **LB83** $17.99

Passion for Israel: *A Short History of the Evangelical Church's Support of Israel and the Jewish People*
—Dan Juster

History reveals a special commitment of Christians to the Jews as God's still elect people, but the terrible atrocities committed against the Jews by so-called Christians have overshadowed the many good deeds that have been performed. This important history needs to be told to help heal the wounds and to inspire more Christians to stand together in support of Israel.

978-1936716401   **LB78** $9.99

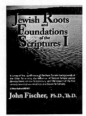

Jewish Roots and Foundations of the Scriptures I & II
—John Fischer, Th.D, Ph.D.

An outstanding evangelical leader once said: "There is something shallow about a Christianity that has lost its Jewish roots." A beautiful painting is a careful interweaving of a number of elements. Among other things, there are the background, the foreground and the subject. Discovering the roots of your faith is a little like appreciating the various parts of a painting. In the background is the panorama of preparation and pictures found in the Old Testament. In the foreground is the landscape and light of the first century Jewish setting. All of this is intricately connected with and highlights the subject—which becomes the flowering of all these aspects—the coming of God to earth and what that means for us. Discovering and appreciating your roots in this way broadens, deepens and enriches your faith and your understanding of Scripture. This audio is 32 hours of live class instruction - audio is clear and easy to understand.

9781936716623   **LCD03 / LCD04** $49.99 each

The Gospels in their Jewish Context
—John Fischer, Th.D, Ph.D.

An examination of the Jewish background and nature of the Gospels in their contemporary political, cultural and historical settings, emphasizing each gospel's special literary presentation of Yeshua, and highlighting the cultural and religious contexts necessary for understanding each of the gospels. 32 hours of audio/video instruction on MP3-DVD and pdf of syllabus.

978-1936716241   **LCD01** $49.99

The Epistles from a Jewish Perspective
—John Fischer, Th.D, Ph.D.

An examination of the relationship of Rabbi Shaul (the Apostle Paul) and the Apostles to their Jewish contemporaries and environment; surveys their Jewish practices, teaching, controversy with the religious leaders, and many critical passages, with emphasis on the Jewish nature, content, and background of these letters. 32 hours of audio/video instruction on MP3-DVD and pdf of syllabus.

978-1936716258   **LCD02** $49.99

The Red Heifer *A Jewish Cry for Messiah*
—Anthony Cardinale

Award-winning journalist and playwright Anthony Cardinale has traveled extensively in Israel, and recounts here his interviews with Orthodox rabbis, secular Israelis, and Palestinian Arabs about the current search for a red heifer by Jewish radicals wishing to rebuild the Temple and bring the Messiah. These real-life interviews are interwoven within an engaging and dramatic fictional portrayal of the diverse people of Israel and how they would react should that red heifer be found. Readers will find themselves in the Land, where they can hear learned rabbis and ordinary Israelis talking about the red heifer and dealing with all the related issues and the imminent coming and identity of Messiah.

978-1936716470   **LB79** $19.99

The Borough Park Papers
—Multiple Authors

As you read the New Testament, you "overhear" debates first-century Messianic Jews had about critical issues, e.g. Gentiles being "allowed" into the Messianic kingdom (Acts 15). Similarly, you're now invited to "listen in" as leading twenty-first century Messianic Jewish theologians discuss critical issues facing us today. Some ideas may not fit into your previously held pre-suppositions or pre-conceptions. Indeed, you may find some paradigm shifting in your thinking. We want to share the thoughts of these thinkers with you, our family in the Messiah.

Symposium I:
The Gospel and the Jewish People
248 pages
978-1936716593   LB84 $39.95

Symposium II:
The Deity of Messiah and the Mystery of God
211 pages
978-1936716609   LB85 $39.95

Symposium III:
How Jewish Should the Messianic Community Be?
978-1936716616   LB86 $39.95

On The Way to Emmaus: *Searching the Messianic Prophecies*
—Dr. Jacques Doukhan

An outstanding compilation of the most critical Messianic prophecies by a renowned conservative Christian Scholar, drawing on material from the Bible, Rabbinic sources, Dead Sea Scrolls, and more.

978-1936716432   LB80 $14.99

Yeshua *A Guide to the Real Jesus and the Original Church*
—Dr. Ron Moseley

Opens up the history of the Jewish roots of the Christian faith. Illuminates the Jewish background of Yeshua and the Church and never flinches from showing "Jesus was a Jew, who was born, lived, and died, within first century Judaism." Explains idioms in the New Testament. Endorsed by Dr. Brad Young and Dr. Marvin Wilson. 213 pages.

978-1880226681   **LB29** $12.99

Gateways to Torah *Joining the Ancient Conversation on the Weekly Portion*
—Rabbi Russell Resnik

From before the days of Messiah until today, Jewish people have read from and discussed a prescribed portion of the Pentateuch each week. Now, a Messianic Jewish Rabbi, Russell Resnik, brings another perspective on the Torah, that of a Messianic Jew. 246 pages.

978-1880226889 **LB42** $15.99

Creation to Completion *A Guide to Life's Journey from the Five Books of Moses*
—Rabbi Russell Resnik

Endorsed by Coach Bill McCartney, Founder of Promise Keepers & Road to Jerusalem: "Paul urged Timothy to study the Scriptures (2 Tim. 3:16), advising him to apply its teachings to all aspects of his life. Since there was no New Testament then, this rabbi/apostle was convinced that his disciple would profit from studying the Torah, the Five Books of Moses, and the Old Testament. Now, Rabbi Resnik has written a warm devotional commentary that will help you understand and apply the Law of Moses to your life in a practical way." 256 pages

978-1880226322 **LB61** $14.99

Walk Genesis! Walk Exodus! Walk Leviticus! Walk Numbers! Walk Deuteronomy!
Messianic Jewish Devotional Commentaries
—Jeffrey Enoch Feinberg, Ph.D.

Using the weekly synagogue readings, Dr. Jeffrey Feinberg has put together some very valuable material in his "Walk" series. Each section includes a short Hebrew lesson (for the non-Hebrew speaker), key concepts, an excellent overview of the portion, and some practical applications. Can be used as a daily devotional as well as a Bible study tool.

Walk Genesis!	238 pages	978-1880226759	**LB34**	$12.99
Walk Exodus!	224 pages	978-1880226872	**LB40**	$12.99
Walk Leviticus!	208 pages	978-1880226926	**LB45**	$12.99
Walk Numbers!	211 pages	978-1880226995	**LB48**	$12.99
Walk Deuteronomy!	231 pages	978-1880226186	**LB51**	$12.99
SPECIAL! Five-book Walk!		5 Book Set **Save $10**	**LK28**	$54.99

Good News According To Matthew
—Dr. Henry Einspruch

English translation with quotations from the Tanakh (Old Testament) capitalized and printed in Hebrew. Helpful notations are included. Lovely black and white illustrations throughout the book. 86 pages.

978-1880226025	**LB03**	$4.99
Also available in Yiddish.	**LB02**	$4.99

They Loved the Torah *What Yeshua's First Followers Really Thought About the Law*
—Dr. David Friedman

Although many Jews believe that Paul taught against the Law, this book disproves that notion. An excellent case for his premise that all the first followers of the Messiah were not only Torah-observant, but also desired to spread their love for God's entire Word to the gentiles to whom they preached. 144 pages. Endorsed by Dr. David Stern, Ariel Berkowitz, Rabbi Dr. Stuart Dauermann & Dr. John Fischer.

978-1880226940   **LB47** $9.99

The Distortion *2000 Years of Misrepresenting the Relationship Between Jesus the Messiah and the Jewish People*
—Dr. John Fischer & Dr. Patrice Fischer

Did the Jews kill Jesus? Did they really reject him? With the rise of global anti–Semitism, it is important to understand what the Gospels teach about the relationship between Jewish people and their Messiah. 2000 years of distortion have made this difficult. Learn how the distortion began and continues to this day and what you can do to change it. 126 pages. Endorsed by Dr. Ruth Fleischer, Rabbi Russell Resnik, Dr. Daniel C. Juster, Dr. Michael Rydelnik.

978-1880226254   **LB54** $11.99

eBooks Now Available!
All books are available as ebooks for your favorite reader

Visit www.messianicjewish.net for direct links to these readers for each available eBook.

God's Appointed Times *A Practical Guide to Understanding and Celebrating the Biblical Holidays* – **New Edition.**
—Rabbi Barney Kasdan

The Biblical Holy Days teach us about the nature of God and his plan for mankind, and can be a source of God's blessing for all believers–Jews and Gentiles–today. Includes historical background, traditional Jewish observance, New Testament relevance, and prophetic significance, plus music, crafts and holiday recipes. 145 pages.

English	978-1880226353	**LB63**	$12.99
Spanish	978-1880226391	**LB59**	$12.99

God's Appointed Customs *A Messianic Jewish Guide to the Biblical Lifecycle and Lifestyle*
— Rabbi Barney Kasdan

Explains how biblical customs are often the missing key to unlocking the depths of Scripture. Discusses circumcision, the Jewish wedding, and many more customs mentioned in the New Testament. Companion to *God's Appointed Times*. 170 pages.

English	978-1880226636	**LB26**	$12.99
Spanish	978-1880226551	**LB60**	$12.99

Celebrations of the Bible *A Messianic Children's Curriculum*

Did you know that each Old Testament feast or festival finds its fulfillment in the New? They enrich the lives of people who experience and enjoy them. Our popular curriculum for children is in a brand new, user-friendly format. The lay-flat at binding allows you to easily reproduce handouts and worksheets. Celebrations of the Bible has been used by congregations, Sunday schools, ministries, homeschoolers, and individuals to teach children about the biblical festivals. Each of these holidays are presented for Preschool (2-K), Primary (Grades 1-3), Junior (Grades 4-6), and Children's Worship/Special Services. 208 pages.

978-1880226261	**LB55**	$24.99

Passover: *The Key That Unlocks the Book of Revelation*
—Daniel C. Juster, Th.D.

Is there any more enigmatic book of the Bible than Revelation? Controversy concerning its meaning has surrounded it back to the first century. Today, the arguments continue. Yet, Dan Juster has given us the key that unlocks the entire book—the events and circumstances of the Passover/Exodus. By interpreting Revelation through the lens of Exodus, Dan Juster provides a unified overview that helps us read Revelation as it was always meant to be read, as a drama of spiritual conflict, deliverance, and above all, worship. He also shows how this final drama, fulfilled in Messiah, resonates with the Torah and all of God's Word. — Russ Resnik, Executive Director, Union of Messianic Jewish Congregations.

978-1936716210	**LB74**	$10.99

The Messianic Passover Haggadah
Revised and Updated
—Rabbi Barry Rubin and Steffi Rubin.

Guides you through the traditional Passover seder dinner, step-by-step. Not only does this observance remind us of our rescue from Egyptian bondage, but, we remember Messiah's last supper, a Passover seder. The theme of redemption is seen throughout the evening. What's so unique about our Haggadah is the focus on Yeshua (Jesus) the Messiah and his teaching, especially on his last night in the upper room. 36 pages.

English	978-1880226292	**LB57**	$4.99
Spanish	978-1880226599	**LBSP01**	$4.99

The Messianic Passover Seder Preparation Guide
Includes recipes, blessings and songs. 19 pages.

English	978-1880226247	**LB10**	$2.99
Spanish	978-1880226728	**LBSP02**	$2.99

The Sabbath *Entering God's Rest*
—Barry Rubin & Steffi Rubin

Even if you've never celebrated Shabbat before, this book will guide you into the rest God has for all who would enter in—Jews and non-Jews. Contains prayers, music, recipes; in short, everything you need to enjoy the Sabbath, even how to observe havdalah, the closing ceremony of the Sabbath. Also discusses the Saturday or Sunday controversy. 48 pages.

978-1880226742   **LB32** $6.99

Havdalah *The Ceremony that Completes the Sabbath*
—Dr. Neal & Jamie Lash

The Sabbath ends with this short, yet equally sweet ceremony called havdalah (separation). This ceremony reminds us to be a light and a sweet fragrance in this world of darkness as we carry the peace, rest, joy and love of the Sabbath into the work week. 28 pages.

978-1880226605   **LB69** $4.99

Dedicate and Celebrate!
A Messianic Jewish Guide to Hanukkah
—Barry Rubin & Family

Hanukkah means "dedication" — a theme of significance for Jews and Christians. Discussing its historical background, its modern-day customs, deep meaning for all of God's people, this little book covers all the how-tos! Recipes, music, and prayers for lighting the menorah, all included! 32 pages.

978-1880226834   **LB36** $4.99

The Conversation
An Intimate Journal of the Emmaus Encounter
—Judy Salisbury

"Then beginning with Moses and with all the prophets, He explained to them the things concerning Himself in all the Scriptures." Luke 24:27
If you've ever wondered what that conversation must have been like, this captivating book takes you there.

"The Conversation brings to life that famous encounter between the two disciples and our Lord Jesus on the road to Emmaus. While it is based in part on an imaginative reconstruction, it is filled with the throbbing pulse of the excitement of the sensational impact that our Lord's resurrection should have on all of our lives." ~ Dr. Walter Kaiser President Emeritus Gordon-Conwell Theological Seminary. Hardcover 120 pages.

Hardcover	978-1936716173	**LB73**	$14.99
Paperback	978-1936716364	**LB77**	$9.99

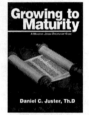

Growing to Maturity
A Messianic Jewish Discipleship Guide
—Daniel C. Juster, Th.D.

This discipleship series presents first steps of understanding and spiritual practice, tailored for the Jewish believer. It's purpose is to aid the believer in living according to Yeshua's will as a disciple, one who has learned the example of his teacher. The course is structured according to recent advances in individualized educational instruction. Discipleship is serious business and the material is geared for serious study and reflection. Each chapter is divided into short sections followed by study questions. 256 pages.

978-1936716227	**LB75**	$19.99

Growing to Maturity Primer: *A Messianic Jewish Discipleship Workbook*
—Daniel C. Juster, Th.D.

A basic book of material in question and answer form. Usable by everyone. 60 pages.

978-0961455507	**TB16**	$7.99

Conveying Our Heritage A Messianic Jewish Guide to Home Practice
—Daniel C. Juster, Th.D. Patricia A. Juster

Throughout history the heritage of faith has been conveyed within the family and the congregation. The first institution in the Bible is the family and only the family can raise children with an adequate appreciation of our faith and heritage. This guide exists to help families learn how to pass on the heritage of spiritual Messianic Jewish life. Softcover, 86 pages

978-1936716739	**LB93**	$8.99

That They May Be One
A Brief Review of Church Restoration Movements and Their Connection to the Jewish People
—Daniel Juster, Th.D

Something prophetic and momentous is happening. The Church is finally fully grasping its relationship to Israel and the Jewish people. Author describes the restoration movements in Church history and how they connected to Israel and the Jewish people. Each one contributed in some way—some more, some less—toward the ultimate unity between Jews and Gentiles. Predicted in the Old Testament and fulfilled in the New, Juster believes this plan of God finds its full expression in Messianic Judaism. He may be right. See what you think as you read *That They May Be One*. 100 pages.

978-1880226711	**LB71**	$9.99

The Greatest Commandment
How the Sh'ma Leads to More Love in Your Life
—Irene Lipson

"What is the greatest commandment?" Yeshua was asked. His reply—"Hear, O Israel, the Lord our God, the Lord is one, and you are to love Adonai your God with all your heart, with all your soul, with all your understanding, and all your strength." A superb book explaining each word so the meaning can be fully grasped and lived. Endorsed by Elliot Klayman, Susan Perlman, & Robert Stearns. 175 pages.

978-1880226360	**LB65**	$12.99

Blessing the King of the Universe
Transforming Your Life Through the Practice of Biblical Praise
—Irene Lipson

Insights into the ancient biblical practice of blessing God are offered clearly and practically. With examples from Scripture and Jewish tradition, this book teaches the biblical formula used by men and women of the Bible, including the Messiah; points to new ways and reasons to praise the Lord; and explains more about the Jewish roots of the faith. Endorsed by Rabbi Barney Kasdan, Dr. Mitch Glaser, & Rabbi Dr. Dan Cohn-Sherbok. 144 pages.

978-1880226797	**LB53**	$11.99

You Bring the Bagels, I'll Bring the Gospel
Sharing the Messiah with Your Jewish Neighbor
Revised Edition—Now with Study Questions
—Rabbi Barry Rubin

This "how-to-witness-to-Jewish-people" book is an orderly presentation of everything you need to share the Messiah with a Jewish friend. Includes Messianic prophecies, Jewish objections to believing, sensitivities in your witness, words to avoid. A "must read" for all who care about the Jewish people. Good for individual or group study. Used in Bible schools. Endorsed by Harold A. Sevener, Dr. Walter C. Kaiser, Dr. Erwin J. Kolb and Dr. Arthur F. Glasser. 253 pages.

English	978-1880226650	**LB13**	$12.99
Te Tengo Buenas Noticias	978-0829724103	**OBSP02**	$14.99

Making Eye Contact With God
A Weekly Devotional for Women
—Terri Gillespie

What kind of eyes do you have? Are they downcast and sad? Are they full of God's joy and passion? See yourself through the eyes of God. Using real life anecdotes, combined with scripture, the author reveals God's heart for women everywhere, as she softly speaks of the ways in which women see God. Endorsed by prominent authors: Dr. Angela Hunt, Wanda Dyson and Kathryn Mackel. 247 pages, hardcover.

978-1880226513   **LB68** $19.99

Divine Reversal
The Transforming Ethics of Jesus
—Rabbi Russell Resnik

In the Old Testament, God often reversed the plans of man. Yeshua's ethics continue this theme. Following his path transforms one's life from within, revealing the source of true happiness, forgiveness, reconciliation, fidelity and love. From the introduction, "As a Jewish teacher, Jesus doesn't separate matters of theology from practice. His teaching is consistently practical, ethical, and applicable to real life, even two thousand years after it was originally given." Endorsed by Jonathan Bernis, Dr. Daniel C. Juster, Dr. Jeffrey L. Seif, and Dr Darrell Bock. 206 pages

978-1880226803   **LB72** $12.99

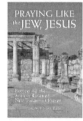

Praying Like the Jew, Jesus
Recovering the Ancient Roots of New Testament Prayer
—Dr. Timothy P. Jones

This eye-opening book reveals the Jewish background of many of Yeshua's prayers. Historical vignettes "transport" you to the times of Yeshua so you can grasp the full meaning of Messiah's prayers. Unique devotional thoughts and meditations, presented in down-to-earth language, provide inspiration for a more meaningful prayer life and help you draw closer to God. Endorsed by Mark Galli, James W. Goll, Rev. Robert Stearns, James F. Strange, and Dr. John Fischer. 144 pages.

978-1880226285   **LB56** $9.99

Growing Your Olive Tree Marriage *A Guide for Couples from Two Traditions*
—David J. Rudolph

One partner is Jewish; the other is Christian. Do they celebrate Hanukkah, Christmas or both? Do they worship in a church or a synagogue? How will the children be raised? This is the first book from a biblical perspective that addresses the concerns of intermarried couples, offering a godly solution. Includes highlights of interviews with intermarried couples. Endorsed by Walter C. Kaiser, Jr., Rabbi Dan Cohn-Sherbok, Jonathan Settel, Dr. Mitchell Glaser & Natalie Sirota. 224 pages.

978-1880226179   **LB50** $12.99

In Search of the Silver Lining *Where is God in the Midst of Life's Storms?*
—Jerry Gramckow

When faced with suffering, what are your choices? Storms have always raged. And people have either perished in their wake or risen above the tempests, shaping history by their responses…new storms are on the horizon. How will we deal with them? How will we shape history or those who follow us? The answer lies in how we view God in the midst of the storms. Endorsed by Joseph C. Aldrich, Ray Beeson, Dr. Daniel Juster. 176 pages.

978-1880226865 **LB39** $10.99

The Voice of the Lord *Messianic Jewish Daily Devotional*
—Edited by David J. Rudolph

Brings insight into the Jewish Scriptures—both Old and New Testaments. Twenty-two prominent Messianic contributors provide practical ways to apply biblical truth. Start your day with this unique resource. Explanatory notes. Perfect companion to the Complete Jewish Bible (see page 2). Endorsed by Edith Schaeffer, Dr. Arthur F. Glaser, Dr. Michael L. Brown, Mitch Glaser and Moishe Rosen. 416 pages.

9781880226704 **LB31** $19.99

Kingdom Relationships *God's Laws for the Community of Faith*
—Dr. Ron Moseley

Dr. Ron Moseley's Yeshua: A Guide to the Real Jesus and the Original Church has taught thousands of people about the Jewishness of not only Yeshua, but of the first followers of the Messiah.
In this work, Moseley focuses on the teaching of Torah -- the Five Books of Moses -- tapping into truths that greatly help modern-day members of the community of faith. 64 pages.

978-1880226841 **LB37** $8.99

Mutual Blessing *Discovering the Ultimate Destiny of Creation*
—Daniel C. Juster

To truly love as God loves is to see the wonder and richness of the distinct differences in all of creation and his natural order of interdependence. This is the way to mutual blessing and the discovery of the ultimate destiny of creation. Learn how to become enriched and blessed as you enrich and bless others and all that is around you! Softcover, 135 pages.

978-1936716746 **LB94** $9.99

Train Up A Child *Successful Parenting For The Next Generation*
—Dr. Daniel L. Switzer

The author, former principal of Ets Chaiyim Messianic Jewish Day School, and father of four, combines solid biblical teaching with Jewish sources on child raising, focusing on the biblical holy days, giving fresh insight into fulfilling the role of parent. 188 pages. Endorsed by Dr. David J. Rudolph, Paul Lieberman, and Dr. David H. Stern.

978-1880226377 **LB64** $12.99

Fire on the Mountain - *Past Renewals, Present Revivals and the Coming Return of Israel*
—Dr. Louis Goldberg

The term "revival" is often used to describe a person or congregation turning to God. Is this something that "just happens," or can it be brought about? Dr. Louis Goldberg, author and former professor of Hebrew and Jewish Studies at Moody Bible Institute, examines real revivals that took place in Bible times and applies them to today. 268 pages.

978-1880226858   **LB38** $15.99

Voices of Messianic Judaism *Confronting Critical Issues Facing a Maturing Movement*
—General Editor Rabbi Dan Cohn-Sherbok

Many of the best minds of the Messianic Jewish movement contributed their thoughts to this collection of 29 substantive articles. Challenging questions are debated: The involvement of Gentiles in Messianic Judaism? How should outreach be accomplished? Liturgy or not? Intermarriage? 256 pages.

978-1880226933   **LB46** $15.99

The Enduring Paradox *Exploratory Essays in Messianic Judaism*
—General Editor Dr. John Fischer

Yeshua and his Jewish followers began a new movement—Messianic Judaism—2,000 years ago. In the 20th century, it was reborn. Now, at the beginning of the 21st century, it is maturing. Twelve essays from top contributors to the theology of this vital movement of God, including: Dr. Walter C. Kaiser, Dr. David H. Stern, and Dr. John Fischer. 196 pages.

978-1880226902   **LB43** $13.99

The World To Come *A Portal to Heaven on Earth*
—Derek Leman

An insightful book, exposing fallacies and false teachings surrounding this extremely important subject... paints a hopeful picture of the future and dispels many non-biblical notions. Intriguing chapters: Magic and Desire, The Vision of the Prophets, Hints of Heaven, Horrors of Hell, The Drama of the Coming Ages. Offers a fresh, but old, perspective on the world to come, as it interacts with the prophets of Israel and the Bible. 110 pages.

978-1880226049   **LB67**   .$9.99

Hebrews Through a Hebrew's Eyes
—Dr. Stuart Sacks

Written to first-century Messianic Jews, this epistle, understood through Jewish eyes, edifies and encourages all. 119 pages. Endorsed by Dr. R.C. Sproul and James M. Boice.

978-1880226612   **LB23** $10.99

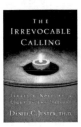

The Irrevocable Calling *Israel's Role As A Light To The Nations*
—Daniel C. Juster, Th.D.

Referring to the chosen-ness of the Jewish people, Paul, the Apostle, wrote "For God's free gifts and his calling are irrevocable" (Rom. 11:29). This messenger to the Gentiles understood the unique calling of his people, Israel. So does Dr. Daniel Juster, President of Tikkun Ministries Int'l. In *The Irrevocable Calling*, he expands Paul's words, showing how Israel was uniquely chosen to bless the world and how these blessings can be enjoyed today. Endorsed by Dr. Jack Hayford, Mike Bickle and Don Finto. 64 pages.

978-1880226346 **LB66** $8.99

Are There Two Ways of Atonement?
—Dr. Louis Goldberg

Here Dr. Louis Goldberg, long-time professor of Jewish Studies at Moody Bible Institute, exposes the dangerous doctrine of Two-Covenant Theology. 32 pages.

978-1880226056 **LB12** $ 4.99

Awakening *Articles and Stories About Jews and Yeshua*
—Arranged by Anna Portnov

Articles, testimonies, and stories about Jewish people and their relationship with God, Israel, and the Messiah. Includes the effective tract, "The Most Famous Jew of All." One of our best anthologies for witnessing to Jewish people. Let this book witness for you! Russian version also available. 110 pages.

English	978-1880226094	**LB15**	$ 6.99
Russian	978-1880226018	**LB14**	$ 6.99

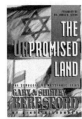

The Unpromised Land *The Struggle of Messianic Jews Gary and Shirley Beresford*
—Linda Alexander

They felt God calling them to live in Israel, the Promised Land. Wanting nothing more than to live quietly and grow old together in the country of refuge for all Jewish people, little did they suspect what events would follow to try their faith. The fight to make *aliyah*, to claim their rightful inheritance in the Promised Land, became a battle waged not only for themselves, but also for Messianic Jews all over the world that wish to return to the Jewish homeland. Here is the true saga of the Beresford's journey to the land of their forefathers. 216 pages.

978-1880226568 **LB19** $ 9.99

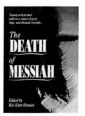

Death of Messiah *Twenty fascinating articles that address a subject of grief, hope, and ultimate triumph.*
—Edited by Kai Kjaer-Hansen

This compilation, written by well-known Jewish believers, addresses the issue of Messiah and offers proof that Yeshua—the true Messiah—not only died, but also was resurrected! 160 pages.

978-1880226582   **LB20** $ 8.99

Beloved Dissident *(A Novel)*
—Laurel West

A gripping story of human relationships, passionate love, faith, and spiritual testing. Set in the world of high finance, intrigue, and international terrorism, the lives of David, Jonathan, and Leah intermingle on many levels--especially their relationships with one another and with God. As the two men tangle with each other in a rising whirlwind of excitement and danger, each hopes to win the fight for Leah's love. One of these rivals will move Leah to a level of commitment and love she has never imagined--or dared to dream. Whom will she choose? 256 pages.

978-1880226766   **LB33** $ 9.99

Sudden Terror
—Dr. David Friedman

Exposes the hidden agenda of militant Islam. The author, a former member of the Israel Defense Forces, provides eye-opening information needed in today's dangerous world.

Dr. David Friedman recounts his experiences confronting terrorism; analyzes the biblical roots of the conflict between Israel and Islam; provides an overview of early Islam; demonstrates how the United States and Israel are bound together by a common enemy; and shows how to cope with terrorism and conquer fear. The culmination of many years of research and personal experiences. This expose will prepare you for what's to come! 160 pages.

978-1880226155   **LB49** $ 9.99

It is Good! *Growing Up in a Messianic Family*
—Steffi Rubin

Growing up in a Messianic Jewish family. Meet Tovah! Tovah (Hebrew for "Good") is growing up in a Messianic Jewish home, learning the meaning of God`s special days. Ideal for young children, it teaches the biblical holidays and celebrates faith in Yeshua. 32 pages to read & color.

978-1880226063   **LB11** $ 4.99